THE
CHRISTIAN'S
TOOLKIT

THE CHRISTIAN'S TOOLKIT

7 ESSENTIAL TOOLS AVAILABLE TO ALL CHRISTIANS

BY

BOB LANKFORD

ISBN: 978-0-578-86098-5

To my faithful wife Deanna and companion over 51 years and counting, and my two children Stephanie and Brian, who have loved me and stood by me through my seminary days and beyond. God has richly blessed me with the most loving family, and I owe them my life. My prayer is that this book will not only bless many Christians but also give glory to our heavenly Father.

TABLE OF CONTENTS

PREFACE

As a child growing up, you found that there are problems in life. At an early age, you found that as you grew, your clothes did not fit anymore. That was a problem. As you continued to grow, people did not always look favorably upon you and called you names. That was a problem. When you learned to drive, and your car quit running, that was a problem. If you live long enough in this world, you will encounter problems.

Dealing with problems in life is not always easy. If your toy breaks, you take it to mom or dad to fix it. If you are old enough to own a car, you will encounter problems. Problems just need to be fixed. Some qualified people are trained to fix problems, whether they are physical or mental. When your car breaks down you take it to a mechanic who has the proper tools to fix your broken car. If you have mental or physical problems, there are trained doctors or nurses qualified to help fix your problem.

As a Christian, you will encounter spiritual problems as well. Who do you go to for your spiritual problems? When your pastor or counselor is not available to help you with your problems, you do have tools that are designed to help you with your problems. Many of those problems are caused by sin, and that requires the Great Physician—the Lord Jesus Christ. What are those tools?

The seriousness of human sin resulted in separation from God and a shame of human life to the extent that any mention of the *"image of God"* in humanity seems inconceivable, if not disrespectful. The infinite love and power of God, however not only made human restoration a possibility but also lead to the redemptive suffering which made it real for those who believe in Christ.

The Christian life is an expression of one's reconciliation with God. Being a part of the Christian community is not an option for believers. Christians are told in Hebrews 10:25, *"not forsaking our own assembling together, as is the habit of some, but encouraging one another."*

Otherwise we would miss the personal meaning and practical changes in our lives when we believe in Christ.

In my opinion, it is a categorical fact that independent human life begins at conception. After a woman's egg is fertilized by a man's sperm, it produces an embryo in the woman's womb. This embryo begins growing immediately and is dependent upon the mother's body to supply the needed nutrients for life. Once a child is born into this world it continues to depend on its mother for nourishment until it reaches adolescence. In the adolescence stage, the child then becomes independent. I emphasize the independent life because the child is no longer dependent upon the mother's body to give it nourishment. Hence, the baby becomes independent.

Having said that, I now step into the spiritual realm. We can most assuredly say that spiritual life begins with spiritual birth. The Bible tells us that unless a person has experienced this "new birth" he has not even begun the Christian life. As Jesus said plainly to the religious leader Nicodemus in John 3:3, *"Truly, truly, I say to you, unless one is born again, he cannot see the kingdom of God."* This just simply means that a man does not become a Christian as a result of his upbringing, his moral effort, his religious affiliations, or any other way except by an experience so profound that Jesus called it being *"born again."*

Once we have been born again, this new birth is followed by a new life. There is no such thing as conversion without change; that is a contradiction in terms. The Apostle Paul put it very clearly in 2 Corinthians 5:17, *"Therefore if anyone is in Christ, he is a new creature; the old things passed away; behold, new things have come."* In other words, the Christian is identified or marked by a quality of life utterly different from the one he lived before he became a Christian.

So, what is the overall distinguishing mark of the Christian? We find the answer further down in Paul's letter to the Colossians in 3:12-14:

> *"So, as those who have been chosen of God, holy and beloved, put on a heart of compassion, kindness, humility, gentleness and patience; bearing with one another, and forgiving each other, whoever has a complaint against anyone; just as the Lord forgave you, so also should you, beyond all these things put on love, which is the perfect bond of unity."*

So, now that you are a new Christian, or returning to the faith, what should you do?

In this book, I offer you seven basic tools to help you grow spiritually in your Christian life or as you renew your faith in God.

You may have been a Christian for many years but wandered away and now you need to put your life back on track. What do you do?

My desire, as you read this book, is that it will enrich your Christian growth daily to be more like Christ and ultimately lead you to a place of service to our Lord and Savior Jesus Christ.

Welcome to the family of God or welcome back to the fellowship with God.

Bob Lankford

PRAYER

"...Lord, teach us to pray..."
(Luke 11:1)

A s we grow in Christ, our relationship with God is one of the most important tools of the Christian life. Prayer is an important tool in every chapter of this book and will play an essential part as you apply each tool. So, now that you are a Christian, how should you pray, and when should you pray, and what do you pray for, to have an effective prayer life? These are important questions, and I am sure you have other questions as well. My desire that this book will help you establish a prayer life that is not only rewarding but brings you to a closer relationship with God.

Let me begin by saying what prayer is not. Prayer is not a one-sided communication with a distant God. Prayer is simply a conversation between you and God, a relationship between you and the Creator. When God created this world, he put man in it so that he could have fellowship with him. He wants you to love him with all your being.

Look at it this way, when you made your profession of faith in Jesus Christ, you became a child of the Almighty God—that same Creator God. This is very much like you would have a relationship with your father or mother. You talk to them regularly. So, as a new Christian, you talk to God just like you talk to your mom or dad and you simply say, "Father I need to talk to you." First of all, you say, "I love you." From that point, you just say what is on your mind or your heart. God loves to hear what you want to say.

The Bible tells us:

> *"You shall love the LORD your God with all your heart and with all your soul and with all your might"* (Deuteronomy 6:5).

He also wants you to know and experience his love and his presence. You see, God is looking for that kind of relationship with you!

So, how do you pray?

Let me make it simple. You see, the disciples, who had been with Jesus for a long time, saw him pray many times. They realized that there was a special connection Jesus had with the Father. They learned to believe in him as a Master in the art of prayer. No one could pray like him. And so, they came to him with a request.

> *". . . one of His disciples said to Him,' Lord, teach us to pray . . ."* (Luke 11:1)

As we grow in the Christian life, the thought and the faith of the Beloved Master in his never-failing prayer life becomes even more precious. The act of prayer is a term you will hear many times in life. The word prayer means intercession, which is a word that means, going to someone in place of someone else. Intercession (prayer), is talking to God in place of or on behalf of someone else. The hope of being like Christ in intercession shows in our hearts. This is what we need to be taught. When we asked Jesus to come into our hearts, that was a prayer. It was a simple prayer, yet at the same time, it is the highest and holiest work to which a person can do. It is fellowship with the Unseen and Most Holy God. It is, simply put, communication with God.

Every new Christian can turn his thoughts toward heaven to speak with his heavenly Father in prayer. It takes no special language, no specific formula, no certain place or posture. No topic is off-limits. A Christian can pray anywhere, any place, any time, about anything that is on his / her mind. Prayer is just between you and God.

Let me offer a suggestion here, and only a suggestion. You might want to get a partner to pray with you. You can do it in person or over the phone or even on the computer. The purpose of having a partner is for accountability. You do not have to share your most intimate requests if they are private, but you can share your basic needs with your prayer partner who can help you pray for those needs.

So, what should I say in my prayer? There are many formulas for prayer as well as good examples in the Bible, including the Lord's Prayer, which Jesus gave us as a model or an outline to follow. These prayers contain four parts. I use the acrostic **A-C-T-S**.

Adoration
Confession
Thanksgiving
Supplication

Adoration to God. Now, this may seem odd to someone raised in the church, but adoration is the essence of worship. Worship is paying a compliment to God or praising him for who he is. There should be a time in prayer where our concentration is on the great attributes of God's character. You could say,

"Lord, I am so overwhelmed with your love today."

"I praise you for your omniscience and may your name be glorified."

"Father, you are so awesome and faithful. You have never let me down."

"Lord, I am so confused right now. Thank you that you see things so clearly, Lord. You know all things."

Beginning a prayer this way is not only appropriate to God's person, but it reminds you of the greatness of the One who hears your prayer.

Confession of sins.

You must be honest in your prayer because honesty is essential for effectiveness. You do not need to parade all my sins before others, but you do need to be clear in private with God. There is a time to be clear about sin with others.

> James 5:16 says: *"Therefore, confess your sins to one another, and pray for one another so that you may be healed. The effective prayer of a righteous man can accomplish much."*

Confession is not just agreeing with God that specific actions are sins, it is also admitting my need for him.

Thanksgiving to God.

When you pray, God wants to hear how appreciative you are about the blessings he has given you. He is eager to hear your gratefulness. Nothing is too large or too small to thank him for in your prayer. You can thank him for your life, your salvation, the air you breathe, each beat of your heart, his love, etc.

Supplication.

God concerns himself with your needs. On any given day, you have a basketful of problems—personal, professional, and relational. How foolish you are when you fail to turn to him to enlist his help. Sometimes it is a good idea to get on your knees and plead with God for your requests. An example would be praying for the salvation of a family member or a special friend. Another example would be if you have a financial need and you need to plead with God to meet that need. Again, nothing is too great or too small for God. Your health or a family member's health is important to them and you as well. It doesn't hurt to beg God for his help.

In all reality, God wants to hear about every area of your life no matter how complicated or trivial your concern may seem to you.

Here is a very crucial point about prayer: it is not a reward that you deserve but it is a privilege given to you by God himself. It is his gift to you, not your gift to him. Let me just say, prayer is a gift of his grace. The only requirement is the Father-child relationship given to all who have received Christ by faith.

> John 1:12 says: *"But as many as received Him, to them He gave the right to become children of God, even to those who believe in His name."*

Any attempt to gain God's ear or refusal to come to him because of sin is to miss the entire point of grace. God the Father, calls you to believe and consent to be loved, heard, and answered even though unworthy of that great position.

Listen, God will answer in his time and in his way. He may keep you waiting for a long time. Or, on the other hand, in his superior wisdom he may determine to answer, not precisely as you had hoped for, but in some other and perhaps a better way. Let me just say, God loves you and knows what is best for you. The Apostle Paul said it this way:

"In the same way the Spirit also helps our weakness; for we do not know how to pray as we should, but the Spirit Himself intercedes for us with groanings too deep for words." (Romans 8:26)

When Jesus was in the Garden of Gethsemane, he went a little bit further out by himself, away from his disciples and he fell on his face and prayed:

"My Father, if it is possible, let this cup pass from Me; yet not as I will, but as You will." (Matthew 26:39)

Jesus' main thought here was God's will. Your prayer is not asking God to do what you want, but it is trying on your part to make your will co-operative with his eternal goodwill.

After you have learned how to pray, what should you pray for? I have already mentioned one acrostic **A-C-T-S**, for a means of offering prayers.

Let me offer another acrostic you can use as a means of prayer. You can use these five elements of prayer that make it easy to remember what to pray for.

8

F
A
C
T
S

This acrostic uses the same letters of the previous acrostic but adds an "**F**" to the front—**F-A-C-T-S**! The "**F**" stands for **faith**. Pray with faith—believing God will answer your prayer. As I mentioned earlier, the "**A**" stands for **adoration**. Praise God for His greatness and love. The "**C**" stands for **confession**. Confess your sins to God. The "**T**" stands for **thanksgiving**. Give thanks to God for all the blessings He has given you. And finally, the "**S**" stands for **supplication**. Ask God earnestly and humbly that He will act according to His will.

This leads to the question of when to pray.

The short answer is anytime! It is a good practice to meet with God at the same time each day as God will be waiting to hear from you if you establish a private time with him. As I previously stated, you can pray anywhere and anytime. But the best time to pray is whenever you can get alone with little or no distractions. The best time is when you can concentrate on praying and listening to God. My suggestion is to designate a time of the day, be it early morning, noon, or late evening—whatever works best for you. Go to a room where you can close the door and spend quality time with God. It is best to establish a quiet time to be alone with God. You can tell someone that you are going to have your Quiet Time or put a note on the outside of the closed door that says, Quiet Time in Progress! Try to make your prayer time the same time each day. God will be expecting to hear from you.

Your prayer time is your time. Take a few moments to pray about your personal prayer life. Ask God to direct you to make the adjustments necessary to develop a meaningful lifestyle of prayer.

So, what should you pray for? A good idea would be for you to make a list of people or things or concerns you want to pray for and place the list in front of you when you pray. You must not follow your lists so rigorously that the practice becomes legalistic, routine, or ritualistic. You see, your prayer must be personal and intimate. Use your list as a general guide to:

Prevent your praying from focusing exclusively on yourself,

Aid your memory so that you do not forget special concerns,

Assign an order of importance to your requests if time is limited.

Plan free periods of prayer so that you can follow the Holy Spirit's leading in many matters, including concerns, praise, and thanksgiving. Just be sensitive to the Holy Spirit and what he leads you to pray for. These can be special times of intercession.

The only tools you need for prayer is the Bible and the Lord's presence. You can also use a hymnal and pick a special hymn that causes you to reflect on someone or something. You can hum a special hymn to help you worship God in prayer.

The Bible is a very important tool to have for your quiet time with God. The reason for that is, the Bible is God's way of talking to you through his Word. I have heard it said that it is more important that God speaks to us than us speaking to God. Spending time reading, studying, memorizing, and meditating on scriptures more frequently will reform your prayer life. Listen to what God may want to say to you as you read and study your Bible.

The Bible is a practical guide for living. It shows you God's will and God's ways. Another important reason for memorizing scripture is so that you will not sin against God. When you know what God says about an activity or a relationship, you can obey what He commands. Meditating on the scriptures you have memorized can also help you observe and do what God says. You should think about these scriptures day and night because they are valuable in shaping and guiding your prayer life. As you use scriptures in prayer, ask the Holy

Spirit to guide you in applying them to a particular situation.

Once you have established a time to spend in prayer, how long should you pray? This will depend on how much time you have set aside for that prayer time. As a rule of thumb, those who pray regularly, usually spend about 30 minutes to an hour for their prayer time. Let me suggest that you spend at least the first 5 minutes in preparation to pray. I would also suggest that you allow the last 5 minutes to ask God to speak to you and to tell you what he wants you to do from this point until the next prayer time. Spend these minutes just waiting on God.

The Bible tells us:

> *"Yet those who wait for the Lord will gain new strength; they will mount up with wings like eagles, they will run and not get tired, they will walk and not become weary."* (Isaiah 40:31)

Waiting on God is not just allowing time to pass by, but it is a spiritual exercise during which, after having spoken to God; he, in turn, speaks to you. Waiting upon God requires our entire being. It is not daydreaming either. You want to be in the most alert frame of mind with all your attention listening to God's voice. God does speak to us through our thoughts, ideas, and impressions.

So why don't more people pray? Just like any worthwhile activity, it is easier to talk about prayer than to pray. It seems nowadays that very few people have time to pray. Prayer is not something that just happens. If anything, we make time to pray. Many obstacles keep us from prayer. If we will just recognize them and admit them, then our battle is half over.

Here are some reasons why some people do not pray:

Prayer is work. The Apostle Paul invited the Roman Christians:

> *"...to strive together with me in your prayers to God..."* (Romans 15:30).

Prayer is the work of diligent Christians. To spend any length of time in prayer is one of the hardest things we do. By that, I mean that it takes all the power of concentration to keep our attention on the business of prayer just for five minutes. Why is it so hard? Prayer, while being a tremendous privilege, is our most powerful weapon against evil. You see, Satan would much rather we engage in any activity other than prayer and he will always make sure there is a truckload of stresses and enticements to divert your attention.

13

You have other resources. It is our sinful nature to attempt to be self-sufficient. The fact of the matter is that you will not trust God until you have no other choice. It is strange that when you have your back up against a wall, you find it easier to pray. Now, you can try to convince yourself that you can do this by yourself. But it is only when you see yourself as dependent on God will you pray. The reality of the situation is that you are dependent on every breath in your lungs each moment. You are much more dependent upon God for the accomplishment of anything of real significance and meaning. As much as it hurts your pride, you cannot do anything of eternal value apart from Christ. Jesus said:

> *". . . for apart from Me you can do nothing"* (John 15:5).

You are committed to your comfort. When you try to stay within your comfort zone and avoid risk or play it safe, you seem to have little need to pray. So, when you step out on the edge of obedience where there are no handrails other than Christ, then prayer will be as natural as breathing. If you stay within your limits and attempt nothing that you know would take an omnipotent (all-powerful) God to accomplish, you will not be moved to pray.

14

You have isolated yourself from others' pain. Here is one of the saddest things about things you may face; you do not pray because you concern yourself with none of the world's great needs. If you will just remove your blinders, and encounter human misery firsthand, and think about what God could do through you, then you would see that God is your only hope of doing anything about the situation, and you will then pray.

You just do not have time. It is rare to find a person who has more time than he knows what to do with. To be honest, you are never going to find time for prayer. You simply must make the time. If you find a way to have prayer occupy a significant place in your life, it will be because you know how desperately, dependent you are on God. When the Apostle Paul challenges you to *". . . pray without ceasing. . ."* he is not asking you to put aside the other activities that demand your time. He is simply pressing you to recognize that God is there with you ready to roll up his sleeves, so to speak, and work with and through you.

Every day you will face obstacles that tell you, you just do not have time for God. If that were the case, you might as well say, "I do not have time to breathe," as to say, "I do not have time for prayer." Prayer to the Christian is much like spiritual breathing. Prayer is the most vital activity you do every day. There are several reasons why prayer is essential to every Christian.

Interaction with each other is essential to any relationship. For two people to get to know one another, they must take time to communicate. In daily communication with each other, they learn something about each other. Jesus promised you:

> *"If you abide in Me, and My words abide in you, ask whatever you wish, and it will be done for you"* (John 15:7).

Oftentimes you will act as though God does not exist, unconscious of his presence. Although this does not affect his unwavering attitude toward you, it certainly affects your attitude toward him. It robs you of the joy of his fellowship, the counsel of his wisdom, and the sense of security that comes from his strength. One of the most valuable resources from heaven is prayer. Jesus teaches in Matthew 7:7:

> *"Ask and it will be given to you; seek, and you will find; knock, and it will be opened to you."*

I mentioned earlier to make a list of your prayer requests. Let me offer a suggestion or two of ways to make that list. Here is an example of a handmade Prayer List:

		Prayer	List	
Day/Date	Name/Item	Description		Update
Fri 1/1/21	Myself	Deeper Bible Study		
Sun 1/17/21	My Church	Growth Program		
Mon 1/18/21	Sally	Salvation		Saved-1/31/21
Fri 1/22/21	Mom	Heart Problem		
Wed 2/3/21	Our Nation	Healing		
Sat 2/6/21	Jones Family	Loss of Father		Funeral-2/10/21

You can find many examples by just typing in a search for "Prayer Lists." Or you can simply get a piece of lined notebook paper and make your own. It does not have to look like this.

You can also make a prayer list for certain days like the sample below where you can fold it to show only the day you are praying. You do not necessarily have to pray for the same thing every day. You may want to pray for a different organization or prayer challenge or events on certain days.

You can make your prayer list from a plain piece of paper like this one on the following page:

THE CHRISTIAN'S TOOLKIT

Day / Date	Request	Date Ans.
1.		
2.		
3.		
4.		

The point is to make a list so that you will remember to pray. It does not have to be like these examples but just make a list. Write it on a blank piece of paper for that matter. Again, the point is to make the list for yourself. You can make up your design or look online for examples.

Is prayer important? Absolutely! It is very important. Things happen to you every day. You are presented with obstacles every day and you can easily say that you do not have time to pray. You might as well say you do not have time to breathe as to say you do not have time to pray. You see, prayer is very much like spiritual breathing. So, prayer is the most vital activity you do each day.

Can you afford to neglect prayer? I mentioned earlier that prayer is communication with God. How else would you get to know someone without communicating with them? If you are married, you spent a lot of time getting to know the person before you ever even considered the possibility of marriage. The communication you did has led you to where you are today.

Did you know that heaven is full of resources available to you if you will only ask? Jesus said:

> *"Ask, and it will be given to you: seek, and you will find; knock, and it will be opened to you."*
> (Matthew 7:7)

God certainly wants to bless you with everything he can pour out upon you. However, he is just waiting for you to ask. James tells us:

> *"...You do not have because you do not ask." We must remember to ask in faith to experience all God has for us."* (James 4:2)

Prayer is the key to peace of mind. The Apostle Paul says:

> *"Be anxious for nothing, but in everything by prayer and supplication with thanksgiving let your requests be made known to God. And the peace of God, which surpasses all comprehension, will guard your hearts and your minds in Christ Jesus."* (Philippians 4:6-7)

Let me sum this chapter up by saying that God looks for people who pray. God looks for people whom the Holy Spirit can use—people of prayer. There are just too many wonderful benefits in prayer. The Apostle Paul also told us in 1 Thessalonians 5:17:

"Pray without ceasing."

Please do not misinterpret this verse. It does not mean to pray continuously every minute of every day. No, I believe he is saying to pray for a particular thing each time you pray, whether you pray often each day or just each day. Just make it a matter of priority to pray that prayer each time you pray.

Does God answer prayers? Absolutely!

Let me give you an example of how God answered one of my prayers.

While I was at seminary studying for my divinity degree, I was working part-time with the seminary maintenance department. A man came to the seminary looking for some short part-time help doing some wiring at some apartments. I had little knowledge of electrical work but a buddy of mine said, "I'll teach you all you need to help with this, and it will only take me five minutes." Well, I volunteered based on what he told me and sure enough, he did teach me in five minutes. I continued to work with him for a little over two weeks until we were done.

One of the drawbacks I encountered was a condition called "Trigger Thumb." I had been twisting wires so long that one of the tendons in my thumb developed a knot on it which caused my thumb to lock in the open position. I went to the seminary doctor and he informed me I needed to see a hand specialist. I did that and he informed me that surgery would be needed to fix the problem.

Deanna and I began to worry because we did not have the money to pay my $200.00 deductible. We made this a matter of immediate prayer. Within two days, we received a letter from my wife's former employer back home. He told us that their business had been going very well and just thought we could use some extra cash and included a check for, you guessed it, $200.00. Yes, it was a quick answer to prayer. However, not all prayers are answered that quickly. My point is, God does answer prayer.

That does not mean your prayers will be answered that quickly either. But if you are diligent and faithful in your prayer life, God will answer your prayers.

Let me give you another example of having a prayer partner or friend to pray with.

When Deanna and I had moved to Ft. Worth to attend seminary, we were waiting for the sale of our house back home to sell and close.

In the meantime, we were renting an apartment in Ft. Worth and our rent was coming due and our home had sold, but we continued to wait for a closing date. After we closed, we would be in the position to pay rent with no problem. However, the timeline was not working out for us and we started praying that the closing would be very soon. We received notice of the closing date, but it was going to be well after our rent would be due.

I shared the prayer request with a fellow student and good friend whom we prayed with often. Without any hesitation, he dismissed himself momentarily and returned to the living room where we were talking and he presented me with a 100-ounce bar of silver, worth over $600.00 at that date and time. I told him I could not accept that from him, and he said it was his honor to help us. We prayed again for the Lord's guidance and were given a feeling of peace about taking the gift.

My friend said that once the house was sold, we could pay it back by just purchasing another 100-ounce bar of silver, therefore there was no interest or note to sign. We made the traditional gentleman's agreement by shaking hands and proceeded the following day to cash-in the bar of silver for cash so we could pay the rent.

After we closed on our house, we took some of the equity we received and bought another 100-ounce bar of silver, then took it back to my friend.

Here is what he said that was so awesome.
God had laid upon his heart to help us and at the
same time, he laid upon our heart to accept the
gift under the conditions my friend laid out.

My point here is that sharing prayers with
friends or even relatives will often lead to
immediate answers. Again, I want to say that
God sometimes does not answer that quickly,
but it is sure awesome when he does.

What a mighty God we serve!

THE CHRISTIAN'S TOOLKIT

BIBLE STUDY

"Study to show thyself approved unto God, a workman that needeth not to be ashamed, rightly dividing the word of truth." 2 Timothy 2:15 (KJV).

"Be diligent to present yourself approved to God as a workman who does not need to be ashamed, accurately handling the word of truth." 2 Timothy 2:15. (NASB)

W hat do I mean by study? Does that mean that I have to go to school? No, not at all! I am not referring to going back to school with teachers and books. The word *study* simply means to "be diligent, be zealous." As a military soldier would be equipped with a weapon, the Christian soldier is equipped with his weapon—the Bible. Also, as prayer was the tool for communication with God, the Bible is the tool God uses to communicate with us. God has given us his

Word to be read, studied, understood, enjoyed, applied, and shared. It is meant to be one of our greatest joys because, through Scripture, we get to know our Creator and his will for our lives.

Notice at the beginning of this chapter above, I used the King James Version and the New American Standard Bible to quote the passage from 2 Timothy. I did this for two reasons: (1) I memorized this verse in the KJV and, it is easier for me to remember the verse this way. Besides, I like the word *"study"* when it refers to reading the Bible. (2) The New American Standard Bible is the one I currently use for bible study and it presents this verse in a manner that emphasizes more how God tells us to be *"diligent"* in our study of the Bible.

A Christian is a worker within the church who diligently studies the Word of God, seeking to apply it to his own life. To study the Bible means to read and re-read it and then contemplating what it says. Bible study, however, begins with a prayer asking God to speak to you. This again emphasizes the need for prayer. You will recall that God speaks to us through the Bible. That is why it is called the Word of God. It is a powerful tool that plays a central role in our relationship with Jesus Christ. For our lives to be a productive and effective spiritual life, we must develop a consistent time of interacting with the Bible. Spending time in his Word is something that might take time, especially early in your Christian life. When you sit down with God's Word, you read it and reflect on it. The Bible has proven to be an invaluable tool for cultivating a relationship with Jesus Christ.

Over time, God is communicating with you through his Word, hence, Bible study will become much of your growth as a Christian. As you do grow, the Bible becomes your manual, containing the blueprint for meaning and significance.

Let me take a moment here to discuss the Bible as it exists today. Without going into the complete background of how the Bible came into existence, let me say that when I became a Christian, I was given the King James Version Bible. As I mentioned, I learned to memorize verses from the KJV Bible, and to this day when I recall a verse, it is generally from the KJV. As I grew spiritually, more versions of the Bible became available, such as the Living Bible, the New International Version, the New American Standard Bible, the New King James Version, etc. Suffice it to say numerous versions of the Bible are available today. So, which one should you get? That is a good question. If you are at the beginning of your journey with Christ, you will find that using one of the modern translations of the Bible will help. I would suggest a study Bible first, and the NIV or NKJV have good study Bibles in print. I have several different versions in my library and use them for comparison. If you notice at the beginning of this book, I chose the New American Standard Bible for quoting, unless otherwise stated, as I believe the NASB compares closest to the original language. This is my opinion, of course.

Let me offer this tip: start your reading in the New Testament. Now, this is not to mean that the Old Testament should not be read, but that the New Testament is easier to read. Later, you will find the Old Testament to be fascinating and extremely helpful. Let me also suggest that you begin your study with one of the four gospels. Starting with Matthew or Luke will give you a more in-depth look at the birth of Jesus.

Reading the Bible is sometimes a difficult task. For instance, the wording or the phrasing of words seem hard to follow. To make your reading easier, spend some moments in prayer asking the Holy Spirit to open your spiritual eyes and ears to what God may be saying to you. The more you read the Bible, the stronger your faith will be.

I mentioned earlier that the Bible is important in your prayer time. When you are reading the Bible, you want to listen for God to speak to you. Again, this is why having a quiet time set aside to pray or talk to God, your quiet time is also important for listening to God.

When you pray, ask God to speak to your heart and reveal what he wants to say to you. You can just simply say, "Father, as I read your Word, I ask that you quiet my heart and speak to me. Reveal to me what you would have me to know. Make your message clear and concise. I open my ears and my heart to you."

I was introduced to a book on Discipleship by a pastor friend of mine and it is called **"Discipleship Essentials – a guide to building your life in Christ,"** by Greg Ogden. I found it quite rewarding and the following process of Bible study is taken from that book.

> "The process of studying the Bible begins with six investigative questions that a good reporter might use in gathering information to write a story:
>
> **Who? (2) What? (3) Where? (4) When? (5) How? (6) Why?**
>
> Once the truth has been revealed, its meaning can be explored and the application to your life is possible. Below is an outline that provides more detail than you could ever follow in one sitting—but it does give you a good idea of the three-step study process.

Observation (What does it say?)

If we take obedience to God seriously then we must find out what God is saying. The first step is to observe exactly what is in the text before we jump to our preconceived ideas.

Overview

Skim material with a view to its main themes.

Note the context of the passage and background if necessary.

Reread in a different translation and look for differences.

Look for main thought divisions—read the passage in paragraphs.

Ask Six Investigative Questions

Who are the main characters, and how are they described?

Notice a description of God, Jesus, and/or the Holy Spirit.

Consider how (or if) the character or personality of the author relates to the passage.

Notice any supernatural beings mentioned.

Notice any human characters mentioned.

What is happening?

List key verbs, commands given by and to whom, promises, conditions implied in text or context, local customs mentioned, the flow of conversation.

Where do the events occur?

How many miles from one place to another? Is this place significant for other events?

When do the events occur?

How long does each event take?

What can be learned from the mention of rulers, ages of characters, the lapse of time, genealogies, cultural differences?

Are there clues about the historical background or season of the year?

Why do the events occur?

How do the events happen?

Summary

Write down the main thrust of the passage. This may become the main thought that you want to develop.

Make notes on unsolved problems as you go through the text. These may be solved in the process of understanding, or you may have to consult reference works such as commentaries, study Bibles, dictionaries, or atlases.

BOB LANKFORD

Interpretation (What does it mean?)

Interpretation aims to bring out the meaning of the passage for the people whom it was written and for us today.

Definitions

What do the terms, phrases, and sentences mean?

What are modern equivalents?

List any surprising terms used, as well as figures of speech—similes, metaphors, puns, plays on words, hyperbole.

Relationships

Why this phrase, word, or idea?

Why did the author say it here?

What relationship does one thought have to another?

Implications

What is the full significance of the statements?

Beware of spiritualizing or allegorizing.

Application (What does it mean to me?)

Cultivate a voice of the Spirit.

Apply the main point to your life.

What has already been a part of my thinking? What is new to me?

What requires a change of thought?

Where do I need a change in my behavior?

What can I do now?

Set long- and short-range goals for behavior. Have a plan. Break down your change of behavior or things you want to know into steps. For example: get counseling, get suggestions for reading, set goals in behavior change, ask someone to hold you accountable.

Assert your will.

What principles are relevant if the historical situation is no longer relevant?

Apply your knowledge to particular areas.

Attitude and obedience to God; attitude toward self.

Situations and relationships in family life.

Coworkers, employers, subordinates, fellow students.

Teaching, practices, relationships in your home church and other churches, missionary work.

National, political, sociological and economic questions."[1]

---

[1] Ogden, Greg Discipleship Essentials (pp. 42-43). InterVarsity Press. Expanded Edition.

After you have become a Christian, the next thing you must do is feed on the Word of God. The Apostle Peter tells us in 1 Peter 2:2-3,

> *"like newborn babies, long for the pure milk of the word, so that by it you may grow in respect to salvation, if you have tasted the kindness of the Lord."*

> "If we feed on the Word of God, it will be easy to speak to others about the Word of God; and not only that, but we will also be growing in grace the entire time, and others will notice the change in our walk and conversation. So, few Christians grow, because so few Christians study the Bible."[2]

I would suggest that you spend as much time as you can with other Christians so that you can learn as much as you can. Do not hesitate to ask Christian friends about Bible verses that you do not know the meaning of. Join a Bible study group, if you can find one in your church or within your community. When you are in a

---

[2] Moody, Dwight L. How to Study the Bible (Updated, Annotated) (pp. 4-5). Aneko Press. Kindle Edition.

Bible study group, it is an excellent time to ask questions. We all learn by asking questions, so do not be afraid to ask.

You will certainly run into words that are hard to pronounce and you will find verses that are hard to understand. Reading the Bible for some people is more like a duty—that is, if they read it at all. However, when you read the Bible and you see Jesus revealed to you, then you know that you are spending time with the Father and you become so excited you want to know more.

You may find yourself asking a friend if they read the Bible the way you started. This is when you come into contact with people who will tell you that the Bible is out of date and no longer applies to today. They will even say that there is a lot of history in there, but it is not intended for today. D. L. Moody says:

> "you might just as well say that the sun, which has shone so long, is now so old that it is out of date, and that whenever a man builds a house, he doesn't need to put any windows in it because we have a newer light and a better light; we have electric light. But it's not true – nothing can replace the sun's

warm rays of light."[3] Isaiah 40:8 says:

"The grass withers, the flower fades, but the word of our God stands forever."

Everything you read in the Bible is true and you will come up against people who will tell you that it is not. They will even ask you to prove that it is true. Do not fear! The Bible will prove itself if you will let it. Without a doubt, there is living power in it. Listen, the Bible does not need to be defended. It only needs to be read and studied. It is not our place to prove the Bible is true, that is the purpose of the Holy Spirit.

The Bible is the only book inspired by God, and it is filled with what he wants us to understand. To read it is to read a personal message to us, written by God himself. To ignore it is to reject his primary method of communicating with us. God wants us to understand who he is, who we are, how we can be reconciled with him, and how we can live fruitful joyful lives. To that end, God gave us the Scriptures. The more we study the Bible, the stronger we will become as his children.

---

[3] Ibid (p. 7).

When I became a Christian, I had this insatiable desire to read the Bible. I could not seem to get enough of it, and as of today I still cannot. I became more interested in who God is. I just could not get enough of him. He is infinitely loving, merciful, gracious, in control, and powerful. I know that even when I face trouble, he is with me, and the result will be for my good and his glory. Jesus said before he was arrested:

> *"This is eternal life, that they may know You, the only true God, and Jesus Christ whom You have sent." (John 17:3)*

And the Apostle Paul wrote:

> *"that the God of our Lord Jesus Christ, the Father of glory, may give to you a spirit of wisdom and of revelation in the knowledge of Him." (Ephesians 1:17)*

Here is an important verse to memorize or remember:

> *"All Scripture is inspired by God and profitable for teaching, for reproof, for correction, for training in righteousness; so that the man of God may be adequate, equipped for*

every good work" (2 Timothy 3:16-17)

The Protestant Bible in its Physical Form

Describing how the Bible came into its present physical form is a whole book in itself. That being said, let me give as brief an explanation of how we got our Bible. God's revelation through the centuries came in a combination of words and deeds. The Egyptian plagues might have been viewed merely as puzzling accidents of nature had Moses not given their meaning. David's rise to the throne of Israel and his capture of Jerusalem might have been written off as minor tides in the ebb and flow of Middle Eastern politics had not Samuel and Nathan laid bare their true significance. Jesus' crucifixion might have seemed another vengeful Roman execution had he not revealed that he would give his life as a ransom for many.

All this Affirms that a canon of Scripture—an authoritative collection of writings, the teachings of which are binding on believers—is not a luxury which the Church has taken to itself. God made himself known by speaking and acting in history. All along he saw to it that the precise nature of his actions and an accurate account of his words were preserved for his people. These records comprise the canon. The word "canon" means "standard" or "rule." It is the list of authoritative and inspired Scriptures. Having said that, the makeup of the Old Testament is as follows:

Five books make up the **LAW**:

        Genesis
        Exodus,
        Leviticus
        Numbers
        Deuteronomy

Twelve make up the **HISTORY** books:

        Joshua
        Judges
        Ruth
        1st and 2nd Samuel
        1st and 2nd Kings
        1st and 2nd Chronicles
        Ezra
        Nehemiah
        Esther

Five make up the **POETRY** books:

        Job
        Psalms
        Proverbs

Ecclesiastes
Song of Solomon

Five make up the **MAJOR PROPHETS**:

Isaiah
Jeremiah
Lamentations
Ezekiel
Daniel

Twelve make up the **MINOR PROPHETS**:

Hosea
Joel
Amos
Obadiah
Jonah
Micah
Nahum
Habakkuk
Zephaniah
Haggai
Zechariah
Malachi

The makeup of the **New Testament** is as follows:

Four books make up the **GOSPELS**:

Matthew
Mark
Luke
John

One book is in a category of its own, called the **ACTS**:

Acts

Twenty-one books make up the **EPISTLES**:

Romans
1st and 2nd Corinthians
Galatians
Ephesians
Philippians
Colossians
1st and 2nd Thessalonians
1st and 2nd Timothy
Titus
Philemon
Hebrews
James
1st and 2nd Peter
1st, 2nd, and 3rd John
Jude,

One other book is in a category of its own, called **REVELATION**:

Revelation

These are all the books that make up the Protestant Bible. There were other writings similar in nature to the books of both Testaments written during these years. Some of these have been kept and are found in certain versions of the Bible like the Vulgate, which is the official Bible of the Roman Catholic Church. The Old Testament was written in the Hebrew language, except for some small sections written in the Aramaic tongue. The writers of the New Testament used Greek.

What a treasure Christian people have in the Bible! And yet how limited and fragmentary is our knowledge of it. But today as never before every eager student to know the Bible.

Bible study can be done at home and especially at church through Sunday School or Group Bible Studies. I would also suggest finding various bible study books at your nearest Christian bookstore or order them online or maybe you can borrow from a friend or relative. Another help is a good study bible, such as the NIV Study Bible or the NKJV Study Bible. There are many study Bibles available and they make a good source for personal home study. After a few years, you will perhaps venture into buying a bible commentary on the whole bible or an individual book of the bible and begin a library of study guides.

BOB LANKFORD

Why is studying the Bible important? Let me give you this example from the great western stars Roy Rogers and Dale Evans back in the 1950s. Roy said:

> "There is nothing in the world more important than understanding the power of God." He went on to say, "All the trials, temptations and struggles that Dale and I have experienced since becoming Christians have only exercised and increased our faith. I've had to study God's Word and I've had to pray. I've had to give myself completely into his hands."

> I've been getting a lot of mail from kids—boys especially—who ask me if I don't think it's pretty sissy for them to go to Sunday School. I want to say right here and now that it isn't sissy at all. I think that going to Sunday School is one of the best things any child can do. So, go to Sunday School regularly, and learn all you can about the Bible and Christ's teaching— you'll always be glad that you did."

I grew up in a Christian home and went to church on a regular basis. Many of my friends did as well. My parents saw to it that we were in church every Sunday and even Wednesday nights. In high school, I even took a class on Bible. When I was in college, I also took a Religion class. Bible study just seemed to be something I wanted to do. When I grew into adulthood and on my own, I managed to stray away from church, like many people did.

I was well into my adult years when I attended a Lay Renewal Weekend at our church. I found myself in a small group and was asked to graph my spiritual life. I tried hard to show peaks and valleys and tried to explain them. However, the Holy Spirit began to work in me and showed me that I was lost and without Jesus in my life. I basically lied about my spiritual graph. When the group study was done, I made it a point to find my pastor and tell him I was lost and needed to ask Jesus into my life.

My pastor and I got on our knees in his office and I prayed to receive Jesus into my heart. On that day, my life was changed, and a new-found feeling came over me. I could now say with all honesty that Jesus lived in me. The presence of Jesus in my life gave me a much greater desire to study the Scriptures. I found myself studying the Bible every day. I can now proudly say, God does change lives. I hope God has made a

difference in your life that you will spend time
studying his Word.

THE CHRISTIAN'S TOOLKIT

CHURCH MEMBERSHIP

"Not forsaking our own assembling together, as is the habit of some, but encouraging one another . . ." Hebrews 10:25

W hy is church membership important? What is the church? Let me address the second question first. The church is more plainly identified as the body of Christ. It is composed of all true believers in the church.

The English word church came by way of Latin and German from the Greek word *kuriakos* which means, "belonging to the Lord," and appears as *kirche, kirk,* and *church.*[4]

So, here is why church membership is important: As believers, we have our names written in the Lamb's book of life, and that is most important. However, it is also important to commit to a local church where we can give of our resources, serve others, and be accountable.

---

[4]Ashcraft, Morris Christian Faith and Beliefs, (p. 264) Broadman Press.

The Bible does not directly address the concept of formal church membership, but several passages strongly imply its existence in the early church. Acts 2:47 says:

> *"And the Lord was adding to their number day by day those who were being saved."*

This only shows that it is a prerequisite for being added to the church. So, this tells us that someone was keeping a numerical record of those who were saved and thus joining the church. And so today, our churches require salvation before membership simply following this model.

Hebrews 13:17 tells us:

> *"Obey your leaders and submit to them, for they keep watch over your souls as those who will give an account..."*

Church membership is important because it defines the pastor's responsibility. Whom will the pastor give an account except for the members of his church? The pastor is the shepherd of the flock (the church put under his care). As a shepherd is not responsible for all the sheep in the world, the pastor is not responsible for all the Christians in the world, only for those who are under his care. He is not responsible for all the people in his community, only for believers under his leadership—his church members. Membership in a local church is a way of voluntarily placing oneself under the "spiritual authority" of a pastor.

Without church membership, there can be no accountability or "church discipline." 1 Corinthians 5:1–13 teaches a church how to deal with blatant, unrepentant sin in its midst. In verses 12–13, the words *"inside"* and *"outside"* are used about the church body. God only prunes those who are "inside" the church—the church members. How can we know who is *"inside"* or *"outside"* the church without an official membership roll?

For these reasons and more, church attendance, participation, and fellowship should be regular aspects of a believer's life. Weekly church attendance is in no sense "required" for believers, but someone who belongs to Christ should have a desire to worship God, receive His Word, and fellowship with other believers.

Church membership signifies your commitment to believe and live in a biblical, God-honoring way. Many churches require prospective members to sign a statement of faith and a church covenant. Church membership signifies that others can count on you to live according to the commitments specified in a church covenant—living a holy life, attending services, praying for your fellow church members, serving them, loving them, supporting the church's discipline, attending its ordinances (Baptism and the Lord's Supper), growing in truth and love, evangelizing your unsaved friends, giving financially to support the ministry and needs of the church, etc.

The Bible sees local churches as flocks of sheep:

> *"Therefore, I exhort the elders among you, as your fellow elder and witness of the sufferings of Christ, and a partaker also of the glory that is to be revealed, shepherd the flock of God among you, exercising oversight not under compulsion, but voluntarily, according to the will of God; and not for sordid gain, but with eagerness; nor yet as lording it over those allotted to your charge, but proving to be examples to the flock." (*1 Peter 5:3*).*

It is never a good thing for a sheep to go solo looking for green grass. Stray sheep make easy prey. We belong in the safety of a flock. Therefore, membership helps keep us gathered with the other sheep under the protection of the shepherd (pastor). Besides, what kind of pastor does not know which particular sheep the

Master has entrusted to him? Membership helps us keep track of whose sheep we are. The pastor is responsible to graze, gather, guide, and guard his church.

If a local church like the one in Ephesus is a physical body, *"members of one another,"* then each person is a body part—an arm or a leg, a hand, foot, thumb, or toe. A body part detached from the rest of its body is not beautiful or cool. It is quite gruesome. But that is what it looks like for a Christian to refuse to join a local church—an arm flopping around on the ground. Arms do not last long when they are detached from a body. And think of what happens to a church body when you refuse to attach your part, or you violently detached from it as well. We can only take the metaphor so far; but as a Christian, to be what God designed you to be, to be part of the body, you need to figure out which body you are going to be attached to, and then formally, visibly, join that body—by becoming a member of it. Besides, your church body needs you, even if you are a tiny pinky toe or an unseen, uncelebrated pancreas.

I recall the story of a man whom God told to be a big toe. He argued with God and said, "God, I want to be an eye." After some dialogue with God for a few minutes, God finally said to him, "OK, you can be an eye, but you are going to be looking at the world through the end of a sock!"

I know that sounds silly, but the truth of the matter is, oftentimes people will argue with God about the part of the body that God wants them to be. God may want you to be a teacher or a leader of some sort in his church. God often calls men or women to serve him in gospel service. Throughout the Bible, God calls people to serve and they have argued with him.

For example, you might recall that Moses asked God why he wanted him to shepherd his people out of Egypt. That is so much like us. We say to God, "why me" or "who am I to do this?"

Remember what Isaiah said when he saw the Lord in a vision in Isaiah 6:5-7:

> *"Then I said, 'Woe is me, for I am ruined! Because I am a man of unclean lips, and I live among a people of unclean lips; for my eyes have seen the King, the Lord of hosts.' Then one of the seraphim flew to me with a burning coal in his hand, which he had taken from the altar with tongs. He touched my mouth with it and said, 'Behold, this has touched your lips; and your iniquity is taken away and your sin is forgiven.'"*

Jeremiah was another one who told God why he did not feel adequate:

> *"Then I said, "Alas, Lord God!*
> *Behold, I do not know how to*
> *speak, because I am a youth." But*
> *the Lord said to me, "do not say,*
> *'I am a youth,' because everywhere*
> *I send you, you shall go. And all*
> *that I command you, you shall*
> *speak. "Do not be afraid of them,*
> *For I am with you to deliver you,"*
> *declares the Lord. For I am with*
> *you to deliver you," declares the*
> *Lord."* (Jeremiah 1:6-8)

The point here is people often tell God what they want or where they want to go, instead of accepting what God wants. People often go to churches they want to go to, instead of praying for God to lead them where he wants them to go. Believe me, I am much happier serving God where he wants me to be, rather than trying to make universal church my church home.

It sounds big to say that you are a member of the universal church and that you love all Christians in the world. But can you love all Christians in the world equally well? To bear one another's burdens, spur one another on to love and good deeds, consider each other more important than yourselves, bear with one another in love, exhort one another, and all the rest, it seems we need to be together in the same place. It is the people sitting next to you, across from you, two aisles up, four aisles back—the local people—that are the most likely beneficiaries of your love. Local church membership says, *these are the particular saints I'm going to prioritize in my discipling and love—warts and all.*

How does the Bible refer to church membership? The Apostle Paul tells us in 1 Corinthians that the church is *like* a body. He says the church *is* a body. The phrase he uses to describe the individual connectedness is we are "members of the body."

Three things that help us understand why church membership is biblical and important.

1. Membership Reflects What the Church Is

Membership is a reflection of the organic community already existing in the body. Paul says we are a body. Can one part say to the other, "I'm not part of you"? No, it is already a part. But too often we live as if we are separated.

Too many churches or Christian gatherings look like piles of dismembered body parts, not a body knit together as God's agent, his body, his kingdom, at work in the world. To reject the value of membership is to deny what God has already established in fact.

2. The Bible Teaches Covenant Community.

We find in Paul's letters to the church at Corinth, 1 Corinthians 5, that they were putting people out of the body because of immorality. So, Scripture teaches that we can be a part of the body, and we can be apart from the body. It is difficult to get around Scripture when it talks about being brought into the body and also being put out of it.

And yet for most churches, there is no way to put somebody out because they are not even in. While there seems to be flexibility according to various bodies, there is no such thing in the New Testament as a church without some recognition of belonging—of membership in the community.

3. People Need Church Membership.

Finally, we recognize biblical membership matters because people need it. People need membership commitment because they need to be connected to a Christian community. This is not just for the sake of the faith community, but also for the sake of the individual.

Individualist Christianity is a myth and a damaging pursuit. At the end of the day, we are redeemed. We are placed in the body. The Bible specifically says he has redeemed us. He has transferred us. Colossians 1 says, from the domain of darkness into the kingdom of the Son he loves. A kingdom has a king. The king has subjects, and his kingdom has a community together where we function as God's people.

God makes us a part of his larger family when we are born again. But then we should covenant in a local body and live in community with them, agreeing to live by certain established godly principles and standards.

The Bible tells us:

> *"Do not be bound together with unbelievers; for what partnership have righteousness and lawlessness, or what fellowship has light with darkness?"* (2 Corinthians 6:14)

We are simply told not to be attached to those who are not Christians. We are to be members of the body (church).

Membership does not save us. But it enables us to grow and become spiritually mature in Christ. Not only should we be members of the body, but each of us should also be able to express the value of membership. Hopefully, then people will stop squirming when we bring up the topic, but instead passionately embrace the biblical nature of church membership.

A New Community—Called into Being

The disciples had formed a community during the ministry of Jesus. We do not know its exact size. One reference at a time shortly after the resurrection, but before Pentecost, mentions in Acts 1:15:

> "...Peter stood up in the midst of the brethren (a gathering of about one hundred and twenty persons was there together)..."

We are unsure as to how many were women and children. But shortly after that, about a couple of weeks, there was phenomenal growth, but the point is not size. Rather, the point is that the believers were aware that they were a new people, a new community. They met, worshiped, shared food, and shared their property.

A significant thing about the church is that members did not organize this movement, it was not of their planning. They had been called together by Jesus and were held together by their faith in him. This "calling" acknowledged that they were in the group because of his initiative, not theirs. Paul understood this and, although his missionary efforts resulted in numerous congregations, saw the church as the community of those:

> *"...called [by God] as saints..."*
> *(Rom. 1:7).*[5]

The Book of Acts, usually published in Bibles as *The Acts of the Apostles*, is filled with statements about the Holy Spirit's leading the churches and the Christians in their decisions and ministry.

We cannot understand the church apart from the leading and empowering role of the Holy Spirit. Ours is not a faith that merely remembers Jesus who died long ago; rather, it is a living belief that Jesus Christ is living today with us as the Holy Spirit.

The Church on Fellowship

The early Christians clearly emphasized the importance of fellowship. Acts 2:42 says:

> *"They were continually devoting*
> *themselves to the apostles'*
> *teaching and to fellowship, to the*
> *breaking of bread and to prayer."*

---

[5] Ibid, p. 268

Why is Christian fellowship important? The New Testament word for "fellowship," is *koinonia*, and it expresses the idea of being together for mutual benefit. Hebrews 10:24-25 gives us this idea:

> *"and let us consider how to stimulate one another to love and good deeds, not forsaking our own assembling together, as is the habit of some, but encouraging one another; and all the more you see the day drawing near."*

Two reasons fellowship with other believers is important are because it helps express love to one another and it encourages good works.

Another important reason for Christian fellowship is its impact on unbelievers. Jesus told His disciples in John 13:35

> *"By this all men will know that you are My disciples, if you have love for one another."*

The love Christians have for one another can influence others toward faith in Jesus Christ. Let me also say that fellowship is the ability to pray together. Early believers were committed to prayer, both individually and in groups. For example, James 5:14-16 tells us:

THE CHRISTIAN'S TOOLKIT

> *Is anyone among you sick? Then
> he must call for the elders of the
> church and they are to pray over
> him, anointing him with oil in the
> name of the Lord; and the prayer
> offered in faith will restore the one
> who is sick, and the Lord will raise
> him up, and if he has committed
> sins, they will be forgiven him.
> Therefore, confess your sins to one
> another, and pray for one another
> so that you may be healed. The
> effective prayer of a righteous man
> can accomplish much."*

Christian fellowship is required for communion, or the Lord's Supper (one of the two ordinances of the church). The Lord's Supper does not work the same for an online church. This ancient practice requires time together with other believers to remember the blood and body of Christ.

The Lord's Supper is a reminder of the time Jesus told us to partake of his body and his blood, which is given for you and he reminds us when he took the bread:

> *"This is My body, which is for
> you; do this in remembrance of
> Me. In the same way He took the
> cup also after saying, 'This cup is*

*the new covenant in My blood; do
this, as often as you drink it, in
remembrance of Me."* (1
Corinthians 11:24-25).

Though many believers today do not
recognize the importance of fellowship or local
church involvement, Christian fellowship is
essential to spiritual growth. Many aspects of
our spiritual lives depend on being together with
other believers to encourage, teach, serve, and
share life. Let me conclude that *"fellowship"* is
a word meaning a relationship that is dependent
on more than one individual. It is an
interdependent relationship.

God created us for one reason: to know him
and love him and have fellowship with him.
And originally that is what happened; Adam and
Eve loved God and yet had broken fellowship
with him. They not only lived in a perfect
world, but they had perfect fellowship with their
Creator.

God still loves us, and he still yearns for us
to know him and love him and have fellowship
with him. And he has made this possible by
sending Jesus Christ into the world to give his
life as a sacrifice for us.

The Church on Mission

The primary purpose of the church is not only to gather together to worship him but, to evangelize the lost. For this purpose, I have devoted an entire chapter, so I will only mention evangelism briefly here. This primary purpose does not minimize or reduce the importance of its other functions. Another important purpose of the church is missions. We are told in Acts 1:8:

> *"But you will receive power when the Holy Spirit has come upon you; and you shall be My witnesses both in Jerusalem, and in Judea and Samaria, and even to the remotest part of the earth."*

I discussed prayer in chapter one and prayer is a key to all mission efforts. Many churches participate in honoring weeks of prayers for missions, as well as specific prayer through prayer groups and prayer ministries of the church. Churches pray for missionaries throughout our country and world.

The early church in Jerusalem had qualities and functions that were entirely different than other New Testament churches. Even the second church chronologically mentioned in Acts 2:44-47, the church in Antioch, did things quite differently than the first church in Jerusalem. Therefore, by the conclusion of the New

Testament, it was obvious that each church had unique characteristics that were different from the others.

The new missionary church made its first major transition as it emerged from Palestine and spread throughout the Mediterranean world. The apostle Paul became a missionary to the Gentile world. With help from Barnabas and a local network of coworkers, many of them women, he evangelized Asia Minor and southern Greece and eventually reached Rome.

Several factors brought growth to the faith. From the beginning laypeople—both men and women—conducted the largest part of missions. Congregations grew in homes used as churches. As multitudes entered the churches, the need for outreach to others was much reduced, and most churches shifted from an outward thrust to an inward focus upon themselves. Mission and service became the province of priests, deacons, and, increasingly, monks.

This is all well and good that churches are involved in mission work, but how does it apply to you? An excellent question!

Let me begin to answer that question with the fact that in the New Testament, every believer is spoken of as the "called" of God or the "chosen" of God, or "set apart" by God (Rom. 1:6; 1 Cor. 1:1-2; Eph. 1:1-6, 18; 4:1; 1 Thess. 1:4; 2 Thess. 1:11; etc.).

Why does God call us?

When you became a Christian, it was because God called you into his fellowship. And when he called you, he had a purpose in mind. The purpose is sometimes not revealed to you until you have reached a point in your Christian life when you heard that call. No, it was not an audible call, but it was a call. It is when your spirit and God's Spirit are in tune with each other and God lays that purpose on your heart. If you have not received that call yet, be patient and prayerful.

I recall when God called me into full-time gospel ministry, I was praying, and I felt in my heart that God had a purpose for me, but it was not yet clear. It began to bother me to the point that I went to my pastor and told him that I was feeling a call but did not know what it was. He told me to keep praying and asking God and he would reveal it to me. I do remember my pastor's words exactly. He said, "Be careful because God will answer you!" That stuck in my head for a few weeks until it was just as plain as it could be. I was being called into the gospel ministry. When I surrendered to God that day, I heard him loud and clear, I finally had peace in my heart.

First, the entire Bible bears witness to the truth that God, from eternity, chose to work through His people to accomplish His purpose in the world. He could have worked everything together Himself, but He chose not to do it that way. The Bible records how God called individuals into a special relationship with Himself at the very times He wanted to accomplish His purposes. When they understood His call and responded to Him, God did work through them mightily to accomplish His purposes.

Second, in understanding the call of God in our lives it is important to realize that God did not make us for time, but for eternity. So, God's goal is not time, but *eternity*. This life, then, is to prepare us for eternity. This was God's purpose from before the foundation of the world.

Third, God's goal is therefore to:

> *"...conform us to the image of His Son..."* (Rom. 8:28-30).

Our character is developed in the heart of the relationship with him in our world as he works out in our life his eternal plan of redemption. Suffice it to say, God calls us into a relationship with himself, so in that relationship, we can come to know him and experience his working in us and through us. In that relationship, and only there, does he develop character in us in preparation for an eternity with him? This may sound to you at this time very "heavy." And it is—but it is the heart of the Christian's life!

The entire process of developing such Christlike character in us begins when God calls us to himself, for a relationship of love. This love relationship continues throughout the rest of life, as God develops us, equips us, and takes us with him on his redemptive mission in our world. Therefore, as Jesus called his disciples and said, *"Follow me,"* they immediately left all and followed Him. Jesus knew it was now his assignment from the Father to prepare them for a world mission's task. And, as Jesus fulfilled that work of training them, he will do the same thing for you.

So, why does God call us? It is so we can come to know and experience him mightily working in us and through us, developing in us Christlikeness of character in preparation for an eternity with him. And he does this because he loves us![6]

What is a Call?

We often think of being saved as simply being able to go to heaven when we die. All through the Bible, and especially in the New Testament, salvation is primarily being called

---

[6] Blackaby, Henry Called and Accountable, (pp. 2-4) Woman's Missionary Union

by God to be in a saving relationship with him. As I mentioned earlier, this relationship of love comes through having a relationship with His Son.

Redemption

Our call into that relationship with God is always REDEMPTIVE. The call to salvation is at the same time a call to be on mission with God in our world. Almost from the moment of salvation there comes over the Christian a deep sense of being on mission with the Lord in our world.

We are ALL called. It is so important to realize that every Christian is called by God when they are saved. So, you were also called, at the moment you were saved. You must let the full implication of your salvation work itself out into every area of your life. You are to respond to him as Lord over all your life. For it is he, now who will be working in your life, causing you to want to do his will, and then working in your life to enable you to do it. What an exciting possibility you have awaiting you!

In the entire process of your salvation, God takes the initiative to come to you and let you know what he is doing or about to do. To the disciples Jesus said:

"You did not choose Me but I chose you, and appointed you that you would go and bear fruit, and that your fruit would remain, so that whatever you ask of the Father's name He may give to you." (John 15:16)

This pattern is found every time God is about to do great work in our world, and it is still true today! It is true right now for your life also!

This call of God will always involve some kind of major adjustment in your life to be the person God can use to accomplish His purposes. One of the greatest developments today is the tremendous number of mission volunteers who are leaving all and following Jesus—across America and around the world. God has no other way to reach a lost world, except through those He calls to become His children through faith in his Son. Such love is what God counts on to move us to go with him into our lost world.

Obedience

One final response always accompanies God's call—OBEDIENCE! Once as a child of God you know an initiative of God in your life, you must immediately, and without resistance or discussion, respond obediently to all God is directing you to do. Only then will you experience God's working mightily through your life.

A call always involves the person in the corporate life of the people of God. Your life, as God calls you, will become vitally involved with all the members of your church family. In essence, the call of God is always a call to the whole world through all of his people.[7]

So, where will you go or what will you do from this point? I will suggest you start by making your quiet time or prayer time an emphasis on what or where God is calling you. When you have received that call, then you must be obedient to it. Just remember, God will help you all the way. He has sent his comforter to help you. Put all your faith and trust in him.

You may have prayed to accept Christ in your own home, somewhere on the road, at a revival meeting or crusade, or you could have been saved in the church you have been attending for some time. Wherever you were at the time you asked Jesus to come into your life and save you, the next thing you must do is find a Bible-believing, Bible-teaching church to help you grow spiritually. Is church membership essential? Absolutely! I mentioned the importance of church membership at the beginning of this chapter. Let me also include

---

[7] Ibid, (pp. 8-10)

the fact, that the church will help you grow and, also minister to you during the discipleship growing process.

The Apostle Peter said:

> *"like newborn babies, long for the pure milk of the word, so that by it you may grow in respect to salvation."* (1 Peter 2:2)

While you are still a new Christian or whether you have just been away from God so long that you need a refresher, you need to learn to ween yourself off spiritual milk and start on more solid food from the Word of God. In other words, you need to dig deeper into God's Word and study it more than just reading it. Keep in mind, this is not a quick process. It does take time and that is the reason for being a part of a Bible-believing, Bible-teaching church. The weening process takes time, just like taking a baby off milk takes time. It is a growing process.

Tom Holliday, teaching pastor at Saddleback Church, mentions in an article called *Eight Laws for Spiritual Growth* on www.pastors.com regarding discipleship: "Children grow through developmental stages: First, they learn to breathe, then they learn to eat. Then they learn to walk. Then they learn to talk. No child has ever taken those steps out of order. They are developmental steps.

The same is true in your spiritual life. The order that we have here at Saddleback is all about helping people grow closer and closer to Christ: knowing Christ, then loving Christ, then growing in Christ, then serving Christ, then sharing Christ."[8]

Rick Warren says in his book "The Purpose Driven Life" that:

> "You will never grow to maturity just by attending worship services and being a passive spectator. Only participation in the full life of a local church builds spiritual muscle."[9]

Let me just say that being a part of church membership is a much more spiritually rewarding experience and you will be so glad you became a part. Not only do you have a new family, but they become so much more. They encourage you in your walk with the Lord. Your

---

[8] https://pastors.com/eight-laws-for-spiritual-growth/#:~:text=The%20order%20that%20we%20have%20here%20at%20Saddleback,steps%20to%20spiritual%20growth.%20Spiritual%20growth%20is%20personal.

[9] Ogden, G. (2007), DISCIPLESHIP ESSENTIALS (p. 20) – *A Guide to Building Your Life in Christ* (Expanded ed.) Downers Grove, IL: InterVarsity Press. Retrieved October 7, 2020

church family becomes like a team. You work together, you study together, you worship together, and fellowship together. You will be so glad you became a part of God's family—the church.

BOB LANKFORD

DISCIPLESHIP

"Go therefore and make disciples of all the nations, baptizing them in the name of the Father and the Son and the Holy Spirit, teaching to observe all that I commanded you; and lo, I am with you always, even to the end of the age."
Matthew 28:19-20

When Jesus commanded his disciples to *"go...and make disciples of all the nations..."* (Matthew 28:19), he spoke the mission statement for the church. Jesus simply told his disciples to do what he had done during his three years of ministry. Jesus made disciples by selecting a few into whom he poured his life.[10]

Making disciples today is the process of making sure that the gospel is implanted deeply in the lives of mature believers who serve as links to the future. So, what is discipling? Discipling is a relationship whereby someone intentionally walks along with you as you grow to become a disciple. That person is to

---

[10] Ogden, G. (2007), DISCIPLESHIP ESSENTIALS (p. 20) – *A Guide to Building Your Life in Christ* (Expanded ed.) Downers Grove, IL: InterVarsity Press. Retrieved October 7, 2020

encourage, correct and challenge you in love to grow toward maturity in Christ.

Now that you are a Christian, how do you become a disciple? Jesus was plain when he told his followers what they needed to do:

> "...If anyone wishes to come after Me, he must deny himself, and take up his cross daily and follow Me. For whoever wishes to save his life will lose it, but whoever loses his life for My sake, he is the one who will save it." (Luke 9:23-24)

Jesus does not make following him sound very easy, does he? To the disciples who were hoping to have a special place in the Lord's earthly kingdom, I am sure these words were not what they had bargained for. You see, to deny oneself and take up a cross was not what they had in mind. At that time, a cross was not a pretty sight.

> "So, what does it mean to deny oneself? To deny oneself means a willingness to let go of your

selfish desires and your earthly
security."[11]

This is probably one of the most
misunderstood and misapplied commands of our
Lord. To deny yourself is used in many
important New Testament texts. To deny
oneself is to say, "I do not know the person." To
deny yourself means to deny your self-lordship.
In other words, "Self" is no longer in charge;
God is. Jesus' followers would need to simply
be willing to set aside all their desires to follow
him and spread the gospel.

> "So, what then does it mean for a
> believer to take up his cross? This
> phrase is also misunderstood and
> misapplied. Many people use it to
> refer to enduring an illness or
> disability, a negative experience,
> or bothersome relationship: "This
> job or illness is just a cross I must
> bear." But Jesus' words mean so
> much more than that. This simply
> means you will follow Jesus to the
> death if necessary. Not only that,
> but it means to die to your selfish

---

[11] Barton, B. B., Veerman, D., Taylor, L. C., &
Osborne, G. R. (1997). *Luke* (p. 244). Wheaton, IL:
Tyndale House Publishers.

desires and ambitions. When Jesus used this picture of his followers taking up their crosses, everyone knew what he meant. Death on a cross was a form of execution used by Rome for dangerous criminals. A prisoner would carry his cross to the place of execution; this signified submission to Rome's power. Following Jesus, therefore, meant identifying with Jesus and his followers, facing social and political oppression and expulsion, and no turning back. And this would not be a once-for-all deal— believers would need to be willing to take up this cross "daily" as they faced new situations, new people, new problems."[12]

So, based on that, what does it mean to *follow* Jesus? This applies to all who would want to be disciples and enter his fellowship. Accepting Jesus as your Lord and Savior is only the beginning of discipleship. Following Jesus does not mean walking behind him but taking the same road of self-denial and self-sacrifice. Because Jesus walks ahead, he provides an

---

[12] Ibid, (p.245)

example and stands with his followers as an encourager, guide, and friend.

The Gospel of Mark tells us in chapter 8 that Jesus and his disciples were traveling through the villages around Caesarea Philippi, a city north of the Sea of Galilee. Up to this point in his ministry, Jesus had done and said things that stimulated the question, *"Who is this man?"* So, Jesus asked his disciples, *"Who do you say I am?"* Peter was quick to answer with *"You are the Christ"* (Mark 8:29 and Matthew 16:16). Jesus knew that he would have to suffer many things and be rejected by the elders, chief priests, and teacher of the law and that he must be killed and after three days rise again. He knew he must leave Caesarera Philippi and make his way to Jerusalem. He also knew that he would suffer and die in Jerusalem.

Those were harsh words to Peter's ears, so he replied:

> *"God forbid it, Lord! This shall never happen to You."* (Matthew 16:22)

That did not fit the concept of Messiah to Peter. To him, the Messiah comes in glory and power.

This may not fit into your concept of being a disciple either. You mean, just as Jesus would be crucified and then resurrected, is that what you would have to prepare to do as a disciple?

Mark then says in verse 24 that a disciple must lose his life to save it for Jesus' sake. How do you lose yourself for Jesus' sake? Just how do you lose your life for him? You will have to give up your life to gain it, and what is gained is of greater value indeed for it is eternal. You see, nothing that you can possess or accomplish here on this earth can compare with eternal life with Christ. If you greedily grasp life, refusing to use it to help others, and focus on satisfying your desires apart from God, you will find that you have lost what you tried to keep. You lose eternal life and forfeit the spiritual fulfillment Christ can give. If you invest your life for Christ and his kingdom, you will receive eternal life as well as the satisfaction of serving God on earth. You give up control to God find that he fills your life with himself.

You will recall back in chapter 1 I mentioned the importance of prayer and how it is a tool that is used often throughout this book. That being the case, I want to emphasize the importance of a quiet time for the disciple. Again, from the book Discipleship Essentials, Dr. Ogden gives us a description of how to begin a quiet time regimen.

A daily quiet time is a private meeting each day between a disciple and the Lord Jesus Christ. Let me make this point very clear. It should not be impromptu. You know that you can commune with the Lord on a spur-of-the-moment basis many times each day, but a quiet time is a time we set aside in advance for the sole purpose of a personal meeting with our Lord.

I want to talk a little about this quiet time. It consists of at least three components.

- Reading the Bible with the intent not just to study but to meet Christ through the written Word.
- Meditating on what we have read so that biblical truth begins to saturate our minds, emotions, and wills. *"...you shall meditate on it* [the Book of the Law] *day and night..."* (Joshua 1:8).
- Praying to (communing with) God: praising, thanking, and adoring him as well as confessing our sins, asking him to supply our needs and interceding for others.

Why should a disciple have a quiet time? There are at least three reasons for that:

1. *It pleases the Lord:*

Even if there were no other consequences, this would be a sufficient reason for private daily communion with God.

Of all the Old Testament sacrifices, there was only one that was daily—the continual burnt offering. What was its purpose? It was not to atone for sin but to provide pleasure (a sweet-smelling aroma) to the Lord. The New Testament directs us to continually offer up a sacrifice of praise to God.

> *"...the fruit of lips that give thanks to His name."* (Hebrews 13:15)

It may astonish us to realize that God is seeking people who will do just that:

> *"... for such people the Father seeks to be His worshipers."* (John 4:23)

One indicator of the depth of our relationship with the Lord is our willingness to spend time alone with him not primarily for what we get out of it but for what it means to him as well.

2. *We receive benefits.*

The psalmist had this in mind when he wrote:

"As the deer pants for the water brooks, so my soul pants for You, O God. My soul thirsts for God, for the living God." (Psalm 42:1-2)

And we benefit from a quiet time in several ways:

- *Information.* We learn about Christ and his truths when we spend time with him and his Word. Before we can obey him, we need to know what he commands. Before we can understand what life is about, we need to know what he has taught.

- *Encouragement.* At times we get discouraged. There is no better source for inspiration than the Lord Jesus Christ.

- *Power.* Even when we know what we should be and do, we lack the strength to be that kind of person and do those kinds of works. Christ is the source of power, and meeting with him is essential to our receiving it.

- *Pleasure.* Being alone with the person we love is enjoyable, and as we spend time with Christ, we experience a joy unavailable anywhere else.

3. *Jesus had a quiet time.*

The Gospel of Mark says:

> *"In the early morning, while it was still dark, Jesus got up, left the house, and went away to a secluded place, and was praying there."* (Mark 1:35)

If our Lord found it necessary to meet privately with his Father, surely his example gives us a good reason to do likewise.

So, the question becomes, will you be a mediocre Christian or a growing disciple of Christ? The answer is whether or not you develop the discipline of a daily quiet time.

Once you desire to have a daily quiet time, how do you start? Let me give you seven steps in starting your quiet time.

1. Remember the principle of self-discipline—do what you should do when you should, the way you

should, where you should, and for the correct reasons. In other words, self-discipline is the wise use of your resources (such as time and energy).

2. Set aside time in advance for your quiet time—a daily quiet time should take place each day at the time when you are most alert. For some this will be in the morning, perhaps before breakfast; for others, it will be another time of the day or evening. Though it is not a hard and fast rule, the morning is a preferable time since it begins before the rush of thoughts and activities of the day. An orchestra does not tune its instruments after the concert.

How much time should you spend? This will vary from person to person, but a good plan to follow is to start with ten minutes a day and build up to approximately thirty minutes. This regularly scheduled chunk of time can be a major factor in strengthening self-discipline. Here is a suggestion: pause while reading this and make a decision—now—about when and for how long, beginning tomorrow, you will meet the Lord Jesus Christ for a daily quiet time.

3. Plan ahead—go to bed early enough so that you can awaken in a refreshed condition to meet Christ. The battle for the daily quiet time is often lost the night before. Staying up late hampers our alertness, making us bleary-eyed and numb as we meet the Lord, or else we oversleep and skip the quiet time altogether.

4. Make your quiet time truly a quiet time—Psalm 46:10 speaks to this: *"Cease striving* [Be still] *and know that I am God"* Turn off your radio or television. Find as quiet a place as possible and make sure your location and position are conducive to alertness. Get out of bed. Sit erect. If you are stretched out in bed or reclining in a chair that is too comfortable you might be lulled into drowsiness.

5. Pray as you start your time with God—ask the Holy Spirit to control your investment of time and to guide your praising, confession,

thanking, adorning, interceding, petitioning, and meditating, as well as to help you get into the Bible Open your mind and heart to Scripture.

6. Keep a notebook handy—write down ideas you want to remember and questions you cannot answer. Expression deepens impression— and writing is a good mode of expression.

7. Share your plans and goals with a friend—tell him or her you are trying to develop the discipline of a daily quiet time. Request his or her prayer that God will enable you to succeed with your objectives.

I know that it is difficult to develop the discipline of a daily quiet time. Let me give you two major reasons as to why it is difficult. *First* is the influence of the flesh. Keep in mind that your old nature is opposed to daily quiet time and to every other discipline that would please Christ. The Apostle Paul tells us:

> *"But I say, walk by the Spirit, and you will not carry out the desire of*

the flesh. For the flesh sets its desire against the Spirit, and the Spirit against the flesh; for these are in opposition to one another, so that you may not do the things that you please." (Galatians 5:16-17)

Pray that the Holy Spirit will enable your new nature to overcome your old nature in this battle.

The **second** reason is resistance by Satan. The devil opposes your every effort to please Christ. His strategy is to rob you of daily quiet time joy, to complicate your schedule by keeping you up late at night and making it hard for you to get up in the morning, to make you drowsy during your time with the Lord, to make your mind wander, and otherwise to disrupt your meeting with Christ. Ask the Holy Spirit to restrain the devil.[13]

As a disciple of Christ, what should you be doing regularly? Let me just give you a few things you need to do to become a faithful disciple.

Worship

---

[13] Ogden, G. (2007), DISCIPLESHIP ESSENTIALS (pp. 35-37) – *A Guide to Building Your Life in Christ* (Expanded ed.) Downers Grove, IL: InterVarsity Press. Retrieved October 9, 2020

Once you become a disciple, what next? In the maturing process, a disciple needs to be a part of the church in worship. Why do you need to worship? Very simply, the church is a caring community—a serving, studying, praying, healing community. If it is true that the chief end of man is to glorify God and enjoy him forever, then fundamentally, the church is a worshiping community.

Worship is a state or attitude of spirit. When Christians formally gather together in worship, the emphasis should be on individually worshiping the Lord. Even in a congregation, participants need to be aware they are worshiping God fully on an individual basis.

The nature of Christian worship is from the inside out and has two equally important parts. We must worship:

> *"...in spirit and in truth"* (John 4:23).

Worshiping in the spirit has nothing to do with our physical posture. It has to do with our innermost being and requires several things.

First, we must be born again. Without the Holy Spirit residing within us, we cannot respond to God in worship because we do not know Him.

> *"No one knows the things of God except the Spirit of God."* (1 Corinthians 2:11)

The Holy Spirit within us is the one who energizes worship because He is, in essence glorifying Himself, and all true worship glorifies God.

Second, worshiping in spirit requires a mind centered on God and renewed by the truth. Paul exhorts us to:

> *"...present your bodies a living and holy sacrifice, acceptable to God, which is your spiritual service of worship. And do not be conformed to this world, but be transformed by the renewing of your mind, so that you may prove what the will of God is, that which is good and acceptable and perfect."* (Romans 12:1-2)

Only when our minds are changed, from being centered on worldly things to being centered on God can we worship in spirit. Distractions of all kinds can flood our minds as we try to praise and glorify God, hindering our true worship.

Third, we can only worship in spirit by having a pure heart, open and repentant. When King David's heart was filled with guilt over his sin with Bathsheba (2 Samuel 11), he found it impossible to worship. He felt that God was far from him, and he *"groaned all day long"* feeling God's hand heavy upon him (Psalm 32:3,4). But when he confessed, fellowship with God was restored and worship and praise poured forth from him. He understood that:

> *"The sacrifices of God are a broken spirit; a broken and a contrite heart, O God"* (Psalm 51:17)

Praise and worship toward God cannot come from hearts filled with unconfessed sin.

The second part of true worship is worship *"in truth."* All worship is a response to truth, and that which is the truth is contained in the Word of God. Jesus said to His Father:

> *"Thy word is truth"* (John 17:17).

> *Psalm 119 says, "Thy law is truth"* (v. 142)

> And *"Thy word is true"* (v. 160).

To truly worship God, we must understand who He is and what He has done, and the only place He has fully revealed Himself is in the Bible. Worship is an expression of praise from the depths of our hearts toward a God who is understood through His Word. If we do not have the truth of the Bible, we do not know God, and we cannot be truly worshiping him.

Giving God Glory

Every aspect of the Christian ethic and the Christian life, in general, should be God-oriented rather than man-oriented. The highest motive for the child of God is the desire to glorify God. So, what does *"glory"* actually mean?

The references in the Bible to the glory of God are frequent and varied. It is said that the glory of the Lord filled the tabernacle. Exodus 40:34 says:

> *"Then the cloud covered the tent of meeting, and the glory of the LORD filled the tabernacle."*

Leviticus 9:23 says:

> *"Moses and Aaron went into the tent of meeting. When they came out and blessed the people, the glory of the LORD appeared to all the people."*

Isaiah 6:3 says:

"...the whole earth is full of His glory."

The Psalmist said that *"The heavens are telling of the glory of God..."* When the angel of the Lord appeared to the shepherds to announce the birth of the Messiah in Luke 2:9 it says, "And an angel of the Lord suddenly stood before them, and the glory of the Lord shone around them..." These are only a few of the many references to the glory of God in both Testaments.

It is doubtful if the glory of God can operate as an effective motive in our lives unless we have a reasonably clear idea of the meaning of "glory." When the children of Israel used the term *"the glory of God"* they referred primarily to the majesty of God. The dictionary definition of "glory" often describes it as great praise, splendor, or honor. The glory of God is the splendor that comes from him. The glory of God is used in a variety of ways in Scripture. It can refer to God's greatness, his honor, his beauty, his power, and his light. In every case, the glory of God acknowledges the Lord's supreme strength and need to both acknowledge and serve him.

The glory of God is the beauty of His spirit. It is not an aesthetic beauty or a material beauty but, it is the beauty that emanates from His character, from all that He is. James 1:10 calls

on a rich man to *"glory in his humiliation,"*
indicating a glory that does not mean riches or
power or material beauty. This glory can crown
man or fill the earth. It is seen within man and in
the earth, but it is not of them; it is of God. The
glory of man is the beauty of man's spirit, which
is fallible and eventually dies, and is therefore
humiliating—as the verse tells us. But the glory
of God, which is manifested in all His attributes
together, never dies. It is eternal.

Isaiah 43:7 says:

> *"Everyone who is called by My
> name, and whom I have created
> for My glory..."*

In context with the other verses, it can be
said that man "glorifies" God, (*why?*) because,
through man, God's glory can be seen in things
such as love, music, heroism, and so forth—
things belonging to God that we are carrying

> *"...in earthen vessels..."* (2
> Corinthians 4:7).

We are the vessels that "contain" his glory.
All the things we can do can find their source in
him.

> *Whatever we do on this earth, we
> should do to the glory of God.
> "Whether, then, you eat or drink*

*or whatever you do, do all to the
glory of God."* (1 Corinthians
10:31)

Paul wrote to the Corinthians, *"whatever you
do, do it all for the glory of God."* He was not
referring to religious checklists, because it is our
daily lives that illuminate the source of love in
our souls. Life within the love of Christ brings
glory to God from simple acts of kindness to the
big goals we work hard to accomplish with the
talents he has given us.

Biblically, glory is defined as an "opinion,
judgment or view; splendor, brightness; a most
glorious condition, most exalted state." Glory is
definitively linked to light, "a halo appearing
around the shadow of an object." Light simply
is. God *is* glorious. We do not bring glory *to*
God, for God is already glorious.

Matthew 5:14-16 says:

> *"You are the light of the world. A
> city set on a hill cannot be hidden;
> nor does anyone light a lamp and
> put it under a basket, but on the
> lampstand, and it gives light to all
> who are in the house. Let your
> light shine before men in such a
> way that they may see your good
> works, and glorify your Father
> who is in heaven."*

The Christian does not carry a light; he *is* a light, the light of the world. Also, his light is not reflected light, such as the moon. He is an inner light, derived from his union with the One who is the Light of the World. The light that we have comes from God, belongs to him. It should be used to glorify him. We shine only to the degree that we permit the Divine Inner Light to touch and transform our lives. The more fully we let that Light permeate our lives the more we will produce good works.

All good comes from the Father, so our good deeds reflect *His* glory. Through Christ, His light flows through our lives, reflecting the goodness and glory of the Father. We glorify God when we extend grace to others, dedicate time to spend with Him, and worship Him – not just through singing praises, but in the way, we live our daily lives.

So, again I will say that as a Christian disciple, whatever you do in your life, do it *"for the glory of God."* For example, when I write, I write for the glory of God. One statement of purpose for my writers' group is that we all write *"for the glory of God."*

Let me suggest that when men glorify God, they do not add to his glory. You see, his glory is complete or perfect. Even the best and most mature of men, however, can never completely comprehend the glory of God. As we put the glory of God first in our lives, we will understand more fully the nature of that glory. And by our works as Christians, others will be enabled to recognize more clearly the nature of the glory and will be led to praise, honor, or glorify God.

Handling Your Emotions

Face it, being a Christian is not easy, despite what some may say, especially when you feel like the world's worst sinner. Here is what Miles & Maralene Wesner, both authors say:

> "We are not perfect; other people are not perfect; circumstances are not perfect! As a result of these imperfections, we all feel guilts, angers, and frustrations. These feelings can make us miserable."

Unfortunately, we are not born with an automatic feelings controller. We are not given some specific instinct to deal with our moods. That is why learning to handle emotions is one of life's hardest lessons. It is a crucial lesson, however, because disturbing emotions are inevitable. You cannot deny these emotions. You cannot always suppress them, and you certainly cannot always act them out.

> "What then, can you do with disturbing emotions? The answer

is simple: you can learn to channel them. This is a practical solution to many problems. Once a newcomer stood and gazed at the mighty Mississippi. He noted that the river seemed to have shifted its course. A dry bed showed where it had once flowed. A native explained, 'Yes, it has been changed. You see, it is impossible to stop this great body of water. You cannot dam it up or even diminish it, but you can channel it!'

That is the secret to handling emotions. They are an essential part of our lives. They motivate and energize us. Through channeling, the energy these feelings generate can be diverted from evil purposes to beneficial purposes. It can be turned from destructive actions to constructive action. It can be directed from unproductive goals to product goals.

When we face life's crises, it is normal to experience a whole range of emotions. The emotions we experience in such situations are neither good nor bad. They are human. Even Christ experienced these internal conflicts. He was angry, sad, frustrated, and discouraged. The writer of the book of Hebrews tells us about his experience with emotions:

"For assuredly He does not give help to angels, but He gives help to the descendant of Abraham. Therefore, He had to be made like His brethren in all things, so that He might become a merciful and faithful high priest In things pertaining to God, to make propitiation for the sins of the people. For since He Himself was tempted in that which He has suffered, He is able to come to the aid of those who are tempted.' (Hebrews 2:16-18)

It is important to realize that genuine emotions are legitimate, necessary, and even useful. The emotions themselves are not sinful. Instead, it is how we act out how we feel that determines our morality or immorality. It is also important to realize that every emotion has both a positive and a negative side. Our character becomes 'saintly' by understanding our feelings, choosing our responses, and shaping our behavior toward Christlikeness.

We cannot always control events, but we can control our responses to those events. It is not the problems: it is how we face the problems that matter. How can you be a Christian when you feel like a sinner? The answer is grace." (Wesner, 1988)[14]

Overcome Discouragement

Hope for the future is essential. Without it, we give up. We can reverse the adage "Where there's life, there's hope", and say, "Where there's hope, there's life!" The Scriptures speak to this problem in Proverbs 29:18:

---

[14] Wesner, Maralene and Miles (1988), HOW TO BE A SAINT WHEN YOU FEEL LIKE A SINNER (pp.11-15), Nashville, TN, Broadman Press, Retrieved November 3, 2020

"Where there is no vision, the people are unrestrained..."

The NIV says it this way:

"Where there is no vision, the people perish..."

With vision, we can overcome discouragement, even when defeat seems certain. Isaiah 40:29-31 says:

"He gives strength to the weary, and to him who lacks might He increases power. Though youths grow weary and tired, and vigorous young men stumble badly, Yet those who wait for the LORD will gain new strength; they will mount up with wings like eagles, they will run and not get tired, they will walk and not become weary."

Now, this promise does not mean that every battle will be won. But it does not matter how many skirmishes are lost if you win the war. Let me remind you that George Washington and the other generals of the American Revolution won very few battles, but they did win the war.

Babe Ruth may have hit 714 home runs, but he struck out 1,330 times. So, I want to say, do not be discouraged. James 1:2-4 says:

> *"Consider it all joy, my brethren, when you encounter various trials, knowing that the testing of your faith produces endurance. And let endurance have its perfect result, so that you may be perfect and complete, lacking in nothing."*

In essence, James was saying that "Nothing great is easy, and nothing easy is great. If something is hard, that may mean it is worthwhile."

I could go on and on about people who have endured all kinds of setbacks and have overcome them. Overcomers keep holding on. They can do this because they have [*what?*] faith. They believe in the ultimate victory of truth and righteousness. The Apostle Paul said plainly:

> *"I can do all things through Him who strengthens me…And my God will supply all your needs according to His riches in glory in Christ Jesus."* (Philippians 4:13, 19:)

You see, Christ lives in all Christians. And that makes us invincible and assures us of the final victory. Little stumbles along the way become insignificant when you know the outcome. When you watch an old war movie, you do not worry when you see country after country fall. You do not even panic when battle after battle is lost. You are confident because you know the outcome. You are living on this side of victory.

That happens to be the cure for discouragement. No matter what the odds, no matter what the crushed hopes, no matter what the disappointments we know the outcome. We are living on this side of victory. Jesus said:

> *"...In the world you have tribulation, but take courage; I have overcome the world."* (John 16:33)

> *"For whatever is born of God overcomes the world; and this is the victory that has overcome the world—our faith."* (1 John 5:4)

Walking in Obedience

You are a transformed person. The Apostle Paul says:

> *"And do not be conformed to this world, but be transformed by the renewing of your mind, so that you may prove what the will of God is, that which is good and acceptable and perfect."* (Romans 12:2,)

Let me put this process of transformation in very practical terms. We are creatures of habit and habits are practiced ways of thinking, feeling, or acting. They become so much a part of us that they are second nature. For example, do you button your blouse or shirt from top to bottom or from bottom to top? You see, our habits are so well ingrained in our minds that we can master complex behaviors and perform them without conscious thought. Here is my point: do you remember when you first sat behind the wheel of a car? There were so many things to think about—put the key in the ignition, fasten the seat belt, move the seat into position, keep your eye on the speedometer and the rearview and side mirrors—just to name a few. But thousands of hours later we can slip into the car in the dark, find the slot for the key and buckle the seat belt without even thinking.

Life is simply full of good and bad habits. We have habits of thinking, feeling, and acting that both honor God and displease him. To follow Christ is to commit ourselves to put off the old and putting on the new. The Lord desires us to build God-pleasing habits into our character. The word "habits" comes from the Latin word *habitus*. A priest wears a *habitus*, a piece of clothing that represents a commitment to a holy life. We too, are to put on habits that are formed in practice so that godliness is a built-in instinct.

One of the reasons we fail in our attempts to change bad habits is that we do not respect the power of a habit to hold us. Endurance and discipline are key elements in changing habits. Any new habit takes a minimum of three to six weeks to become part of our routine. Most of us get washed out long before that time. We must know the strength of the battle that is ahead so we can call on the Lord's grace for the change.

Our usual approach to change is to stop a habit of thinking, feeling, or acting. We reduce our food intake, we try to stop being critical, we try to stop drinking or smoking. We do fine for a while. We may even think, *I have this licked.* But then our will crumbles, and the former behavior is back, stronger than ever. When you simply stop doing an old behavior without putting a God-pleasing one in its place, you create a vacuum that is filled by an even stronger version of the same problem.

Paul says that we must practice the principle of replacement. When we "put off" we must "put on" as well. The first step is to identify the habit of thinking, feeling, or acting that needs to be put to death or nailed to the cross. Then we must make a searching and fearless moral inventory of ourselves and admit to God ourselves and other people the nature of the wrong. Then we must prepare ourselves to remove all defects of character. The Holy Spirit's transformation will not be complete until we practice the principle of replacement.

God's intent is for you to reflect his image: Ephesians 4:24 says:

> "...put on the new self, which in the likeness of God has been created in righteousness and holiness of the truth."

Athletes often attain their goals by visualizing their success. A high jumper sees the bar and his body safely flying over it. It is the completion of the goal that motivates him toward what he is to become. We are to see ourselves with the defects of character removed from our lives as Jesus shines through so that we are what God intends us to be.

We must be patient with the process. There is no such thing as instant godliness. To live in a way that is contrary to society, we need to commit ourselves to a lifetime of change under the guidance of the Holy Spirit.

The Holy Spirit is God's tailor—he is ready to give us a new set of clothes and discard the old, threadbare wardrobe. But the old way of life dies a slow, bitter, bloody death. It does not want to give up its grip. Yet the new set of clothes are so much more becoming.

Your prayer should be something like this: "Lord, do what it takes, reach as deep as you need, go after the wrong thinking, wrong feelings, wrong behaviors. Go straight to the heart with whatever pain it will take because my desire is to be made over in the likeness of you."

Biblical discipleship is a model of how Christians could and should live their lives in reflection to Jesus' example and His mission. It involves not only a personal faith with God, but sharing that faith with other people, and building up more disciples.

There is an old saying we used to use, and it is still applicable today: "Teach one to reach one." That is being a disciple.

As an example, not only is Bible Study important in your new life as a Christian, but you will want to become an active disciple, serving God as did his followers.

BOB LANKFORD

EVANGELISM

"... you will receive power when the Holy Spirit has come upon you; and you shall be My witnesses both in Jerusalem, and in all Judea and Samaria, and even to the remotest part of the earth." Acts 1:8

J esus intended for the disciples to produce His likeness in and through the Church being gathered out of the world. His ministry was to duplicate many times over in the lives of his disciples. Through them and others like them, it would continue to expand in an ever-enlarging circumference until the multitudes might know in some similar way the opportunity which they had known with the Master. By this strategy, the conquest of the world was only a matter of time, and their faithfulness to his plan.

Just what is evangelism? Let me explain it this way. Evangelism is the spreading of the Christian gospel by public preaching or personal witness. Just imagine if you had the secret of life in the palm of your hands—the answers to all the questions of life. As Christians, we do have that secret—yet it is not a secret at all, but a truth meant to be shared. The sharing of that

truth—the good news of Jesus Christ—is called
evangelism.

There is an urgent need for men and women
to dedicate themselves to the important task of
becoming specialists in soul-winning! God is
real. Heaven is real. Hell is real. The Bible is the
Word of God and it tells us that all those who
have not received Christ as their Savior will
spend eternity in hell—separated from God, in
conscious torment (Luke 16:23-26; John 3:18).

God has given every Christian a job, a
responsibility, a command. Jesus said:

> *"Go into all the world and preach
> the gospel to all creation."* (Mark
> 16:15)

You can obey God's command, or you can
disobey it. But your orders are still to *witness*.

Remember, witnessing is a *command* of God,
not a *leading*. God leads those who are already
obeying His command to a particular *field* of
service. Obey God's command of "GO" in the
Scriptures! You do not stop your car when the
signal light says, "GO!"

Jesus promised the disciples two things in
Acts 1:8. You shall receive *power* and be my
witnesses. The power they were to receive was
divine; the word for power is *dynamis*, where
we get the word dynamite, which is the same
word used of Jesus' miracles in the Gospels. It

is the *Spirit's* power. The role of the apostles is that of *"witness."* In the book of Acts, the apostles' main role is depicted as witnessing to the earthly ministry of Jesus, above all to his resurrection. As eyewitnesses only they were in the position to be guarantors of the resurrection. But with its root meaning of *testimony*, "witness" comes to have an almost legal sense of bearing one's testimony to Christ. Witnessing is to be the main task of the whole church in the whole world throughout the whole church age.

The Christian disciple is to go into all the world, *"...even to the remotest part of the world."* Sharing the gospel is the central activity of the church and each disciple is to be a witness. In other words, we are to take the message of Jesus to "every unsaved person" in the world.

Matthew added to that Christ's promise in Matthew 28:20:

> *"...and lo, I am with you always, even to the end of the age."*

Finally, Jesus said that witnessing was to be done:

> *"...in Jerusalem, in Judea, in Samaria..."* before the *"...remotest part of the earth."*

The disciples are to witness, not consecutively from one place to another, but simultaneously in every part of the earth.

After the resurrection, Jesus appeared to disciples when they were gathered in Jerusalem discussing the news of the resurrection. It was here that Jesus showed them his hands and his feet, and he ate a piece of broiled fish to convince them that it was him. Then he reminded them that before the crucifixion he had foretold what would happen to him; his death and resurrection had fulfilled the Scriptures. Then he gave them the content of their message—and ours—to a lost world.

Jesus then said:

> *"...Thus it is written, that the Christ would suffer and rise again from the dead the third day, that repentance for forgiveness of sins would be proclaimed in His name to all the nations, beginning from Jerusalem."* (Luke 24:46-47)

This is the point Jesus was making to the disciples. *"You are witnesses of these things,"* referring to what he had just said. Let me just give you four distinctives the church must do:

1. *Gospel verification.* We are to set forth the testimony of Scripture to Christ,

and we are to show how all things which Scripture says concerning him either have been or will be fulfilled.

2. *Gospel events or Gospel deeds.* We are to bear witness to Christ's unique sufferings, his atoning death, and his triumphant resurrection. These facts constitute the heart of the gospel.

3. *Gospel conditions.* Jesus said that repentance is to be preached in his name among all nations.

4. *Gospel benefits.* Forgiveness of sin may be obtained by all who are willing to repent.

In immediate connection with the content of our testimony, Jesus gave the promise of the Holy Spirit, which would provide the power for witnessing:

> *"And behold, I am sending forth the promise of My Father upon you; but you are to stay in the city until you are clothed with power from on high."* (Luke 24:49)

Notice that he explicitly commanded the disciples to wait until the Holy Spirit had come before they began their witnessing ministry.

Jesus' instruction to wait for the Holy Spirit is significant. It indicates beyond all question that we will not, even cannot, obey the Great Commission apart from the Spirit's power.

Here is the heart of their testimony. Without a door even being opened, the risen Lord suddenly appeared among the assembled disciples and he showed them his wounded hands and side—the visible evidence of his atoning work. Then he commanded them to go with this testimony, even as his Father had sent him.

But Jesus does not stop there. He had indicated the content of their testimony and had commanded them to go with it, but he knew they would never go simply under the impulse of a command. So, look what he did in John 20:22:

> *"...He breathed on them and said to them, Receive the Holy Spirit."*

This was a symbolic action looking forward to Pentecost. Jesus' pre-ascension instruction to wait for the empowering of the Spirit was so imperative that no doubt is left: Successful witnessing apart from that empowering is impossible.

So, how does a person evangelize or witness to others? Every new Christian has that question floating around in his mind and that is normal. One must learn how to share his faith with others. There are many methods on how to witness. Let me give you three popular ones:

1. **EE** – Evangelism Explosion
2. **RR** – Roman Road
3. **CWT** - Continuing Witness Training

These are all good methods of witnessing to the lost. I learned from an older program that is no longer in existence, but it was CWT – Continuing Witness Training, which was derived from EE. Some people use diagrams or drawings to illustrate how a lost person needs Christ. Suffice it to say, many churches have their own evangelism teaching or methods to witnessing. Let me just show you some principles for evangelism.

ROLE OF THE HOLY SPIRIT

There are three basic truths of the Holy Spirit's work in bringing lost people to Christ.

1. The Holy Spirit is at work in the lives of all lost people.

    a. The Holy Spirit convicts of sin, of the need for righteousness, and judgment.

    b. The Holy Spirit enables the sinner to see the Savior.

    c. The Holy Spirit brings the sinner out of death into life.

2. The Holy Spirit is at work in the life of the witness to lead and empower the witness to the lost.

3. The Holy Spirit is at work in the life of the lost person during a witnessing experience to convince him what the witness is saying is true. The importance of being empowered by the Holy Spirit in witnessing.

"For our struggle is not against flesh and blood, but against the rulers, against the powers, against the world forces of this darkness, against the spiritual forces of wickedness in the heavenly places." (Ephesians 6:12)

GIVING YOUR TESTIMONY

1. Write out your testimony.

2. List 4 points that should be included in
    your testimony.

3.
    a. My life before I committed to
        following Jesus.
    b. How I realized I needed Jesus.
    c. How I received Jesus.
    d. How Jesus makes my life full and
        meaningful.

4. Learn to present your testimony using
    the four points listed above.

OUR NEED

Embed in your mind the three consequences
of sin. It:

1. Alienates man from God.
2. Degrades man's character.
3. Results in eternal separation (in hell)
    from God.

GOD'S PROVISION

The two results of God's provision are:

1. Victorious living.
2. Eternal life.

Learn the three Bible descriptions of God's nature. God is:

1. Holy.
2. Just.
3. Love.

OUR RESPONSE

Understand the word salvation and how you get it.

The word "save" means "to make whole" and comes from a root meaning "wholeness." It implies setting free that which is bound or healing the wounded and broken. Salvation means deliverance and healing from the destructive power of sin and guilt, and birth into a new nature and life. Nothing short of a miraculous transformation can bring salvation. One must become a new person, and only God can bring about such a birth.

Salvation is not the result of any human effort or achievement. Salvation cannot be gained by education, by human struggle, through culture, or by human capability. The key to salvation is not achieving but receiving. Salvation is God's gift in response to faith (John 1:12). God wants to do for man far more than he deserves or can do for himself.

God loved us so much that he provided a way for us to be made right with him. He came to earth in the person of Jesus Christ, lived a perfect life, died on the cross for each individual's sins, and was resurrected from the dead. He ascended into heaven to rule heaven and earth and to prepare a place for those who believe in him. He did it because of his love. He did this as a gift. And he did the impossible—he made possible our rebirth.

VICTORIOUS LIFE

Learn the four ingredients of a victorious life.
1. Bible (Christian's food).
2. Prayer (Christian's breath).
3. God's family—the church (Christian's environment).
4. Witness (Christian's communication).

OBJECTIONS AND QUESTIONS

There are two principles to use in answering questions and objections.

1. If a listener has an honest question, the gospel presentation will probably answer it.

2. If you maintain a proper spirit and attitude, many objections or questions will not be voiced.

Use these five guidelines when faced with a negative response.

1. Negotiate—do not argue.
2. Avoid emotional confrontation.
3. Accept the other person as an equal.
4. Exercise gentleness.
5. Check your motivation.

How do you introduce the process of evangelism or soul-winning or witnessing with a person? Always look for opportunities to engage in witnessing. One way of starting an introduction is to follow the acrostic:

F
I
R
E

Family

Transition: Do you have any special hobbies?

Interests

Transition: Do you ever feel something is missing in your life?

Religious background

Personal testimony

Transition: Now my life has real meaning.

Exploratory question

Has anything like this ever happened to you?

Transition: God loves us and has a purpose for our lives. The Bible says it this way:

> *"For God so loved the world, that*
> *He gave His only begotten Son,*
> *that whoever believes in Him shall*
> *not perish, but have eternal life."*
> *God's purpose is that we have*
> *eternal life."* (John 3:16)

This is one of the most memorized verses in Scripture and if you haven't memorized it, now would be a good time to do that.

Once you have entered into some personal conversation, this would be a good time to begin presenting or sharing the Gospel.

We might as well face it now—Christian service is demanding, and if we are going to be of any use for God, we must learn to seek first the Kingdom. Yes, there will be disappointments. But of those who do come through and go out to project our life into harvest fields beyond reckoning, there will be increasing joy as the years go by.

We are not living primarily for the present. Our satisfaction is in knowing that in generations to come our witness for Christ will still be bearing fruit through them in an ever-widening cycle of reproduction to the ends of the earth and unto the end of time.

"The world is desperately seeking someone to follow. That they will follow someone is certain, but will he be a man who knows the way of Christ, or will he be one like themselves leading them only on into greater darkness?

This is the decisive question of our plan of life. The relevance of all that we do waits upon its verdict, and in turn, the destiny of the multitudes hangs in the balance."[15]

---

[15] Coleman, Robert E. (1970) THE MASTER PLAN OF EVANGELISM (PP. 125-126), Old Tappan, NJ, Fleming H. Revell Company, Retrieved November 11, 2020

We can and must trust Christ to do every bit of the soul-winning through us that he requires of us, because he is able, and we are not. The apostle Paul said:

> *"Now to Him who is able to do far more abundantly beyond all that we ask or think, according to the power that works within us."*
> (Ephesians 3:20)

While we trust, he works, not according to our power, but according to his.

In another passage, Paul tells us how to receive the crucified life into our experience. He says in Philippians 2:5:

> *"Have this attitude in yourselves which was also in Christ Jesus."*

> "Could anything be easier than to let the mind of Christ possess us? To open the heart to the mind of Christ is to accept his attitude toward death to self that others might live.

> We may practically apply these concepts to the work of soul-winning in two definite ways:

(1) By the power of the indwelling life we die to all consciousness of our ability.

(2) By the power of the indwelling life we also die to all consciousness of our lack of ability.[16]

One of the clearest verses on the discipleship benefits of evangelism is Philemon 1:6 (NIV):

"I pray that you may be active in sharing your faith, so that you will have a full understanding of every good thing we have in Christ."

As you have read in the previous chapter on Discipleship, one of the Lord's greatest needs is for you to evangelize. In other words, the Lord wants you to tell people about him. That is why he gave the great commission to go out into all the world and tell people about him. That does not mean you become an evangelist by trade, although some people do, wherever you encounter people, strike up a conversation that

---

[16] Conant, R. J. (1976). EVERY MEMBER EVANGELISM FOR TODAY (P. 92), New York, NY, Harper and Row, Publishers, Retrieved November 11, 2020

eventually opens the door to talk about Jesus. It could be at work or on the streets or in a foreign land, make it a point to talk about Jesus and how he saved you.

This is a good time to practice your testimony so that you can tell your testimony to lost people and lead them to accept Jesus as their Savior.

I recall going on a trip to New Orleans during Mardi Gras and street witnessing. We had the old nail aprons around our waists and filled with gospel tracts. We would hand them a tract and ask: "Do you know that Jesus loves you?" Oftentimes we would receive responses in the affirmative and other times we would be rejected by people who said, "We came all the way down here to get away from that!" This only proves that evangelism is not easy, but it does take practice and preparation. Do not let evangelism scare you into not witnessing. Do you remember the important phrase Jesus said in Acts 1:8?

> *"But you will receive power when the Holy Spirit has come upon you..."*

If you have not led someone to Christ, I can only describe to you the joy of seeing the transforming power of the gospel newly at work in a person. Experiencing the privilege of leading someone to Christ reminds us of how much more powerful, holy, and merciful God is than we often think him to be.

You see, the Holy Spirit will give you the power to do whatever he wants you to do. As long as you are witnessing in the Spirit's power, nothing can go wrong.

STEWARDSHIP

"As each one has received a special gift, employ it in serving one another as good stewards of the manifold grace of God." 1 Peter 4:10

The fundamental principle of biblical stewardship is that God owns everything. We are simply managers or administrators acting on his behalf. In essence, stewardship expresses our obedience regarding the administration of everything God has placed under our control, which is all-encompassing. Stewardship is the commitment of one's self and possessions to God's service, recognizing that we do not have the right of control over our property or ourselves.

We are all stewards of the resources, abilities (talents), and opportunities that God has entrusted to our care, and one day each one of us will be called to give an account for how we have managed what the Master has given us. In other words, we are called and accountable to God for everything he has given to us. And as a child to whom God has given much, we give back to him from our resources, abilities (talents), and opportunities.

Let me ask you a couple of questions. Have you ever been asked to watch someone's children for a little while? Have you ever been in charge of an office or supervised many employees? Have you ever rented a house or an apartment? Have you ever borrowed a tool of any kind? If you answered yes to any or all of those questions, you were placed as a steward of that property. In other words, you were responsible for the safety or care of those people or items.

So, what is Biblical stewardship? Let me answer that by quoting Genesis 1:1:

> *"In the beginning God created the heavens and the earth."*

As the Creator, God has absolute rights of ownership over all things, and to miss starting here is like misaligning the top button on our shirt or blouse—nothing else will ever line up. Nothing else in the Bible, including the doctrine of stewardship, will make any sense or have any true relevance if we miss the fact that God is the Creator and has full rights of ownership. It is through our ability to fully grasp this and imbed it in our hearts that the doctrine of stewardship is understood.

Now, do not miss this! Everything on earth belongs to God. We were placed here on earth to take manage it. In other words, we are his stewards. That being said, the Psalmist said in Psalm 24:1:

129

"The earth is the Lord's, and all it contains, the world, and those who dwell in it."

We often fail to use God's resources for God's glory. So, we should ask ourselves this question: Am I making decisions and living as if things belong to God or me? The way we live unmistakably declares the answer.

God has never relinquished his title deed to the world, and he never will. The Bible simply teaches that we are to be faithful "stewards" of all that God has made. He has given us basic principles to help us be faithful in this stewardship.

One example is the parable Jesus gave us in Luke 19:12-27. His opening words in verses 12 and 13 were:

"A nobleman went to a distant country to receive a kingdom for himself, and then return. And he called ten of his slaves, and gave them ten minas and said to them, 'Do business with this until I come back.'"

Their assigned work was to be productive in business.

Jesus went on to say that upon the nobleman's return he called the ten servants to account, asking what they had done with the money. Those who had invested wisely received a reward. But one servant, because he was fearful, simply buried the money, then dug it up and gave it back because he knew the nobleman was hard to please and he was afraid he would lose the money. The nobleman reprimanded this servant. In essence, he said:

> *"You vile and wicked slave. Hard, am I? That is exactly how I will be toward you! If you knew so much about me and how tough I am then, why didn't you deposit the money in the bank so I could at least get some interest in it?*

We must never forget that God is the rightful owner of everything, and we are all personally accountable for what we do with his money.

> "Perhaps you are wondering why giving ten percent of one's income has been a common practice among Christians for centuries. A gift of ten percent called a "tithe" in the Bible, first appeared in the time of Abraham, more than four hundred years before God gave the Ten Commandments to Moses. In these early Bible times, God must have given Abraham instructions to tithe.

> We find in the fourteenth chapter
> of Genesis that after his battle with
> the kings, Abraham gave a tenth of
> the spoils of his victory to God's
> priest, Melchizedek. Giving his
> tithe was an act of worship.
> Because of the covenants and
> promises that God made to
> Abraham, it was also an
> expression of his conviction that
> God owned everything he had."[17]

All that being said, we give back to God a portion of what he has generously given to us. I want to talk about some of the ways we give back to God.

GIVING IS WORSHIP

Giving, along with our thanksgiving and praise, is worship. I doubt that there is any subject relating more to stewardship than tithing. Anything that touches our wallets or purses is a very sensitive topic. When a person says, *"It's not the money but the principle of the thing,"* it is the money. It is not strange how uneasy we feel when the matter of giving emerges. Many would rather talk about giving

---

[17] Watts, Wayne (1982). THE GIFT OF GIVING (pp. 22-24), Ft. Worth, TX , NavPress, November 11, 2020

rather than tithing. To some, talk of giving makes them nervous but the idea of tithing arouses feelings of hostility in them.

My wife and I give to the church a designated amount monthly, mainly because we live on Social Security. Before we retired, we gave 10% or tithed on the Sunday following a pay period. When we received money for any other reason, we would give 10% of that the following Sunday. Though we have experienced the joy of giving, the act of making our gift had a little relationship to worship.

A verse of Scripture that has always stood out to me is Deuteronomy 16:16 which says in part:

> *"...they shall not appear before the LORD empty-handed."*

Now that did not mean that I had to give every time I was in church. I took it to mean that if I was given money during the week for my work or a job, I was to tithe on it the following Sunday. Deuteronomy 6:5 says:

> *"You shall love the LORD your God with all your heart with all your soul and with all your might."*

But we know very little about expressing this kind of love through giving. Wayne Watts says again in his book "The Gift of Giving" that "the Lord drew his people to himself at a special place of worship. Though the distances were great, and many had to walk, still they came to express their devotion to God. Continually He sought to build their faith and deepen their character by teaching them how to express their love.

For this reason, Scripture says:

> *"Every man shall give as he is able, according to the blessing of the Lord your God which He has given you'* (Deuteronomy 16:17).

> "This passage reveals two important principles: First, God is leading everyone to give. And second, we are to give as we have been blessed. This same principle is taught by the apostle Paul in 1 Corinthians 16:2":

> *"On the first day of every week each one of you is to put aside and save, as he may prosper."* [18]

Man's heart is so constructed that he will worship what he loves. Invariably, a man will spend time and money on that which he loves

---

[18] Ibid, (pp. 36-37)

deeply. In other words, he will give as he feels spiritually led. There are times when we may be asked to give above and beyond our tithe. That means that there will be times when a special offering will be received for a special purpose. This could be a benevolence offering which is a special offering for a needy person or needy people or it could be a special offering for a revival speaker. It can even be for a mission project or a youth function. Suffice it to say, there are times when a special offering will be received.

What is important here is that we give as God directs us to give. God is not impressed by the size of our gifts, but he is pleased by what we give out of specific obedience. All this demonstrates our love for him. The widow's example in Mark 12:41-44. When we look at this example there are several interesting insights:

When you give to the Lord, He watches you with interest, just as he did in the case of this widow.

When you give, your gift can be a positive example to others. Jesus wanted His disciples to learn from the sacrificial gift of this godly woman.

> "A sacrificial gift means far more to God than gifts given out of surplus income, where the element

of sacrifice and faith is not
required."[19]

The Apostle Paul said in 2 Corinthians 8:12:

*"For if the readiness is present, it
is acceptable according to what a
person has, not according to what
he does not have."*

What this is saying is that either a small or a
large gift can be pleasing to God. Our
motivation for making the gift is what God
looks at. That being said, what is the maximum
one should give? I will answer it this way, the
money we have is not from the government or
our business, but it is from God. So, he alone
determines the maximum. God is our source.

GIVING OUT OF POVERTY

In Wayne Watt's book on "The Gift of
Giving" he says:

"Many Christians do not know
how to start giving because they
are so pressed to pay bills they
have nothing left. Their response
to God's instructions on giving is
'how can we tithe when we are

---

[19] Ibid, (pp. 39-40)

spending more than we are
making?' The answer now as then
is, 'I don't know how, but it
works.' There are many helpful
books written on the subject of
how to manage your finances, but
the best place to start such
management is to give the tithe
first."[20]

Sincere giving will cause our faith to increase, a process that is part of being:

> *"...conformed to the image of His Son..."* (Romans 8:29).

As we give, we find joy and peace—blessings from God which nourish our faith in Him. As we grow in faith we grow in victory over sin and worldliness.

Our giving produces more giving as we mature in our walk with Christ. The Son of God—who created all, owns all, controls all, and lovers all—gave up his heavenly riches and became poor for our sakes, so that we might be rich! If you want an example of giving, meditate on our Lord—the giving Christ!

The more we adhere to God's principles of giving, the more he will pour out his blessings. God is just waiting to exercise his power

---

[20] Ibid, (p.95)

through those who will go "all-out" for Him as they learn and put into practice His principles for giving.

GLORIOUS GIVING

According to Wayne Watt's book "The Gift of Giving" again, he says finally, 'God's principle in giving to us or withholding from us is this: If we sow meagerly, we reap meagerly; if we sow generously, we reap generously. As Paul wrote in 2 Corinthians 9:6-7:

> *"he who sows sparingly will also reap sparingly, and he who sows bountifully will also reap bountifully. Each one must do just as he has purposed in his heart, not grudgingly or under compulsion, for God loves a cheerful giver."*

"God uses the farmer to teach us. If we give little—like the farmer who sows few seeds—we get little in return. If we give much—like the farmer who sows many seeds—we get much more in return.

> We must make our own decision,
> under God's direction, about how
> much we are to give. We are not to
> be pushed or forced, but with a
> willing heart, we should permit
> him to use the amount. The Holy
> Spirit, whose job it is to instruct,
> train, and lead us in our decisions,
> will enlighten our minds. Then our
> gift will be eagerly given—so that
> we can hardly wait to sign the
> check."[21]

We should give with eagerness and joy. God loves a cheerful giver, one who purposes in his heart to give to him then does it gladly. We *"glorify"* God by giving when we acknowledge his presence in or giving. We should not give for the praise of men.

If every professing Christian would tithe, every congregation would be free of financial worries and could begin truly to be:

> *"...the salt of the earth..."*
> (Matthew 5:13).

If every Christian would tithe the church would begin to make an impact on the world that could change it. The church instead is

---

[21] Ibid, (pp. 111-112)

paralyzed. Tithing Christians could make a big difference.

There is ultimately only one reason why every Christian should be a tither: because it is biblical. Tithing was so deeply embedded in the Jewish conscience, that it needed virtually no mention in the New Testament. Tithing was an assumption in Israel when Jesus came on the scene.

I have a book called, **"Tithing A Call to Serious Biblical Giving"** by R. T. Kendall, who is also the author of **"Jonah and Believing God"** is Minister of Westminster Chapel, London, and has been a Southern Baptist pastor in the United States. He gives three reasons for tithing:

1. **You should tithe because of what it will do for the work of God on earth.**

    Malachi 3:10 says*: 'Bring the whole tithe into the storehouse, so that there may be food in My house...'* The same God who claims to own *'...the cattle upon a thousand hills...'*

    (Psalm 50:10) *and to whom the nations are but as '...a drop from a bucket...'*

(Isaiah 40:15) *equally claims his dependence upon his people to return to him what is rightfully his— namely, the tithe.*

'The tithe is the LORD's' (Leviticus 27:30).

As a consequence, the prophet Malachi regarded the withholding of any tithe as robbing God. *'Will a man rob God? Yet you are robbing Me! But you say, 'How have we robbed You? In tithes and offerings'* (Malachi 3:8).

Therefore, 'Bring the whole tithe into the storehouse, so that there may be food in My house...' (Malachi 3:10).

2. You should tithe because of what it would do for God in heaven.

So, what on earth, you may ask, could tithing do for God? Answer: much. How so? Because he loves us so much. God has invested himself in us. God gave his Son. Those who dignify his Son's work on the cross have eternal life. Those 3who look to his Son is declared righteous. This is called justification by faith.

3. We should tithe because of what tithing does for us.

When God says 'now I know' there follows blessing upon blessing. So pleased was God with Abraham that God said in Genesis 22:16-18,

> *"...By Myself I have sworn, declares the Lord, because you have done this thing and have not withheld your son, your only son, indeed I will greatly bless you, and I will greatly multiply your seed as the stars of the heavens and as the sand which is on the seashore; and your seed shall possess the gate of their enemies. 'In your seed all the nations of the earth shall be blessed, because you have obeyed My voice.'"*

Whatever else may be learned from the story of Abraham and Isaac this much is clear: God blesses obedience. We literally cannot outdo the Lord. He waits to bless us. He wants to bless us far more than we want that blessing. But he waits to see whether we take him seriously.

"What tithing does for us, then, is realized at two levels: the natural (or material) and the spiritual. The spiritual is by far the more

142

important, for the very blessing that comes from heaven is essentially spiritual. It is God telling us He is pleased with us."[22]

God gave us all a gift and it is our God-given responsibility to use that gift to glorify him by putting that gift to work for him. You may not know what that gift is but think about it this way; whatever you know or whatever you have been trained for, apply it toward God's work. What are you good at? Then use it to glorify God. I have put on my web page that I write for the glory of God. So, glorify God with your talent or talents. God sometimes blesses us with more than one talent.

---

[22] Kendall, R.T. (1982). TITHING A Call to Serious Biblical Giving (pp. 29, 33-34, 36, 40) (Zondervan edition by special arrangement with Hodder and Stoughton Limited, London, England ed.). Grand Rapids, MI November 18, 2020

SERVICE

"If it is disagreeable in your sight to serve the LORD, choose for yourselves today whom you will serve; whether the gods which your fathers served which were beyond the River, or the gods of the Amorites in whose land you are living; but as for me and my house, we will serve the LORD."
Joshua 24:15

W hat does that mean? I would say that it means to do what he says in a way that makes him look supremely valuable in himself and to submit to him in a way that makes him look delightful.

The kind of service that makes God look valuable and delightful is the kind that serves God by constantly receiving from God. Let us look at 1 Peter 4:11:

"Whoever speaks, is to do so as one who is speaking the utterances of God; whoever serves is to do so as one who is serving by the strength which God supplies; so that in all things God may be glorified through Jesus Christ, to whom belongs the glory and

144

*dominion forever and ever.
Amen."*

God is seen as glorious when all our serving is moment-by-moment receiving from God's supply.

Here is a quote from John Piper:

> "We receive this supply by faith. That is, we trust moment by moment that what we need, in serving him, he will supply ("life, breath, and everything"). This is the opposite of being anxious. Such serving is happy. And it makes God look no less authoritative but infinitely more desirable. This is the glory he means to have. The giver gets the glory."[23]

So, how does one serve the Lord? Let me give you some examples of how you can serve the Lord:

Serve the Lord by Singing

Psalm 100:2 says:

---

[23] John Piper, *What Does It Mean to Serve God?*, (July 2011): https://www.desiringgod.org/articles/what-does-it-mean-to-serve-god

"Serve the LORD with gladness;
come before Him with joyful
singing."

We are commanded not only to serve and
worship God but to do it joyfully. You see,
God's light in our lives is the ultimate cause for
joy and fulfillment, so it is only natural that we
should not only serve him but invite others to do
the same. We can enter into His presence with
praise and glorify His Name knowing that our
service is to the God who has saved us.

Deuteronomy 11:13 says:

> *"It shall come about, if you listen*
> *obediently to my commandments*
> *which I am commanding you*
> *today, to love the Lord your God*
> *and to serve Him with all your*
> *heart and all your soul."*

Your Christian walk is not meant to simply
be a part of your life; it is meant to guide every
aspect of how you live, speak, and act. In
several places throughout the Bible, we are
commanded to love and serve God with all of
our heart, soul, mind, and strength.

Living a life of faith involves the entire
person – your thoughts, your actions, your
beliefs, and everything in between. This is the
way to live a life that reflects a wholehearted
devotion and love for God.

146

1 Corinthians 15:58 says:

> *"Therefore, my beloved brethren,
> be steadfast, immovable, always
> abounding in the work of the Lord,
> knowing that your toil is not in
> vain in the Lord."*

Our work will always yield a good return, so we should be diligent and faithful to remain in God's service our entire lives. We are promised throughout Scripture that God will not abandon us, and one way this proves true is that he will always bring about a result when his Word is preached.

Our part is to simply remain steady in our service. If we remain faithful to his will and his way for us, we can be sure to see the elements of his plans unfold in our lives.

Colossians 3:23 says:

> *"Whatever you do, do your work
> heartily, as for the Lord rather
> than for men."*

Ultimately, we are not serving other people through our work or our service. As Christians, we do what we do to honor God. He is the reason for everything we do, and the motivation that guides our actions. So, by submitting to the lordship of Jesus Christ, we acknowledge Him in our work and service and keep Him at the forefront of our minds as we go.

1 Timothy 1:12 says:

> *"I thank Christ Jesus our Lord, who has strengthened me, because He considered me faithful, putting me into service."*

Becoming a Christian and yielding your life to Christ allows you to serve his purposes. He will always give you the necessary strength to do what he asks of you, and if you remain true to what he has given you, you will be judged faithful and eventually given more and more responsibility in your service. This is an excellent way to grow in your reliance on God by faithfully serving him where he has placed you.

Many of us seek positions of authority and power in this life. This is not the way Christ taught us to live.

Jesus consistently preached that we should serve others and seek their good over our own. Rather than making it the goal of our lives to dominate others, we should instead find ways to serve them and make less of ourselves. This selfless service will be an effective witness for the Gospel because we are simply imitating the sacrificial, service-oriented life of Jesus Christ in everything we do.

In Matthew 20:27 Jesus says:

> *"and whoever wishes to be first*
> *among you shall be your slave."*

Philippians 4:13 is a popular favorite verse with athletes, business professionals, and many Christians today. It simply says:

> *"I can do all things through Him*
> *who strengthens me."*

This typically refers to God's ability to strengthen us for whatever we set our minds to.

Now, while this is true, it is important to read the rest of the letter to the Philippians to more fully understand that God's preparation and provision are sufficient for any life circumstance. We can do anything, go through any trial, and embark on any service in the power and strength of our Father.

So often I have heard people say I would like to sing in the choir, but I do not have a singing voice. Listen, where in the Bible does it say that you must have the voice of an angel to sing praises to God? On the contrary, the Bible tells us that we should make a joyful noise and come before Him singing.

Not only does it tell us *what* to do, it tells us *how* to do it—joyfully! Since I became a Christian, I have attended mostly conservative churches. In most cases, the music reflects that conservatism. However, as I have grown in the Lord, I have learned that music does not have to be played on an organ or piano to be acceptable to the Lord. Many other instruments may be used to worship, and we even find some of them in the Bible.

Psalm 150:2-5 says:

> *"Praise Him for His mighty deeds; Praise Him according to His excellent greatness. Praise Him with trumpet sound; Praise Him with harp and lyre. Praise Him with timbrel and dancing; Praise Him with stringed instruments and pipe. Praise Him with loud cymbals; Praise Him with resounding cymbals."*

Singing and making noise to the Lord is a great way to serve with gladness. Next time you say you do not have the voice to sing—I challenge you to think again because the Lord gave you that voice to praise Him.

Serve the Lord by Teaching

This happens to be another excuse I have heard hundreds of times—I cannot teach! I do not know how to teach. So, I would say that a person has never taught and therefore does not feel capable. I would add to that, that a person does not teach because he has never tried to teach.

We teach and lead because God has called us to do so. For thousands of years, God has asked and equipped teachers to participate in the work of helping others come to know God and live as people of faith. These teachers and leaders have come in many shapes and forms, from many backgrounds, and with many levels of ability. But each has somehow heard a call to teach and has responded.

You may not even realize that you responded to a call. You may think you merely answered a plea for help, or just knew it was your turn to help teach a class! God's call can come in many ways:

- through the voice of a friend
- through prayerful discernment
- from the challenge of a sermon
- by identifying your spiritual gifts
- upon seeing a need and responding
- through the strong movement of the Holy Spirit
- even by a seeming accident as you "fall" into teaching.

Why do we teach? This is an excellent question. Just read the story of Moses' call to leadership in Exodus 3:1–4:17. Notice some of Moses' feelings and concerns that you might have experienced when first asked to teach or lead. God's call to you may not be as flashy as Moses' call through a burning bush, but God's invitation to you and God's promise of support is just as strong as they were in biblical times.

Just like Moses, your first reaction to a call or invitation may have been reluctance or fear. That is normal. When God gives us a task, it can seem overwhelming and we may feel ill-equipped. Moses even had the gall to argue with God and pointed out all of his shortcomings. God assured Moses that his gifts were sufficient, and that help would arrive when needed. Like Moses, we can be assured that God will use whatever skills we have and that we will find the help we need to be an impactful teacher or leader.

God does not call us and then leave us alone. In fact, as a teacher and spiritual leader, you have the promise that God will be with you. Story after story in the Bible tells us that God wants to be in a relationship with us and to be present for us at all times. For example, God said to Moses in Exodus 3:12:

"…Certainly I will be with you…"

God promises to help. Then God send Aaron to help Moses and told him in Exodus 4:15:

> *"You are to speak to him and put
> the words in his mouth; and I,
> even I, will be with your mouth
> and his mouth, and I will teach
> you what you are to do."*

Jesus even promised his followers that the
Holy Spirit would be with them. He said in John
14:14-16:

> *"If you ask Me anything in My
> name, I will do it. If you love Me,
> you will keep my commandments. I
> will ask the Father, and He will
> give you another Helper, that He
> may be with you forever."*

And when giving the Great Commission to
his followers as he was ascending to heaven,
Jesus promised that he would be with them
always (Matthew 28:19-20).

You can trust that God's Spirit is present
with you in the classroom, enabling you to
accomplish things you could not do on your
own. You can also trust that God's Spirit is
guiding the participants in what they hear and
where and how they are called to respond.

A wise teacher once told a group of people
who were learning how to teach that "God goes
before me into every classroom I enter. God is
present in that room before, during, and after I
teach. I don't have to do it all." God is already

present and working in the lives of the people you lead. God will continue to work within them long after you are no longer around. Thanks be to God!

Serve the Lord by Leadership

Cheryl Bachelder is the CEO of Popeyes Louisiana Kitchen, Inc., and she admits to not being particularly gifted in the specific ways her church asked her to serve. While she may not have found joy helping with the kids' ministry, when a later church asked her to help with developing a roadmap, she jumped at the chance.

"During her keynote at the 2019 Pushpay Summit conference, Cheryl dug into the importance of servant leadership, pulling takeaways from her recent book, *Dare to Serve: How to Drive Superior Results by Serving Others.* And the thing is, she doesn't shy away from applying business best practices to the church in a leadership context. She believes the Church would benefit greatly if more lay members brought their years of marketplace experience to the building up of their local ministry."

She went on to say:

"…leadership is not just a matter of strong management principles and book smarts. It is a stewardship responsibility—you are responsible for the people entrusted to your care.

That being said, have you thought about what people say about being under your leadership? Would people say you were the best boss they ever had, or would they be glad upon hearing that you got a new calling?

Servant leaders do not worry about the answer to that question. The leaders with the strongest results and the happiest teams are those who mirror Jesus' age-old leadership style." Whether it's Cheryl or another strategy expert with a copy of *Dare to Serve* in their back pocket, someone in your congregation knows how to apply wise marketplace principles to your ministry. That person might be retired, working, or a few years from college and eager to donate their time and skills. *Tap into your*

> *community. And use your people*
> *to propel your church forward.*"[24]

One of the greatest compliments people can pay Christians is to view them as examples for other Christians to follow. The apostle Paul paid that compliment to the Christians in Thessalonica in 1 Thessalonians 1:7-8:

> *"so that you became an example*
> *to all the believers in Macedonia*
> *and in Achaia. For the word of the*
> *Lord has sounded forth from you,*
> *not only in Macedonia and*
> *Achaia, but also in every place*
> *your faith toward God has gone*
> *forth, so that we have no need to*
> *say anything."*

Their pattern of Christian living was a model worthy of imitation by other Christians. They were living examples of the Christlike life.

The primary model for all Christians is Jesus Christ himself. The apostle Peter gives us the example to follow when he said:

---

[24] Steve Johnson, *Practical Servant Leadership for the Church,* (January 2020): https://pushpay.com/blog/practical-servant-leadership-for-church-leaders/ - Pushpay

156

> *"For you have been called for this*
> *purpose, since Christ also suffered*
> *for you, leaving you an example*
> *for you to follow in His steps."* (1
> Peter 2:21)

Plain and simple, Jesus came to serve. He further emphasized that in Mark 10:45 when he said:

> *"For even the Son of Man did not*
> *come to be served, but to serve,*
> *and to give His life a ransom for*
> *many."*

Jesus dramatically illustrated his servant lifestyle for his disciples. He washed their feet at their last meal together before his arrest and crucifixion. He wanted them to learn unmistakably a basic lesson of servanthood. Jesus said in John 13:12-15:

> *"So when He had washed their*
> *feet, and taken His garments and*
> *reclined at the table again, He*
> *said to them, "Do you know what I*
> *have done to you? You call Me*
> *Teacher and Lord; and you are*
> *right, for so I am. If I then, the*
> *Lord and the Teacher, washed*
> *your feet, you also ought to wash*
> *one another's feet. "For I gave*

you an example that you also
should do as I did to you."

All Jesus' followers were to serve by providing ministry in his name. The title *diakonos* (meaning - servant) applied to every Christian, but the apostle Paul also uses it in a special sense for specific church leaders (Philippians 1:1; 1 Timothy 3). The translators chose not to translate literally in those situations but to make a new English word *deacon* out of the Greek word for servant. So, deacons carry both the name of Christ and the name of the servant.

You may not think you can serve in a certain capacity, but listen, with the Spirit's help, you can do almost anything. You will be surprised how much he will use you.

You might even be nominated to serve on a committee or as a teacher or counselor. God will use you. I have seen God use children to read the Bible in a class or even in a worship service. I know that because I was asked to do that very thing. Just make yourself an instrument that God can use and he will find a way to use you.

BOB LANKFORD

CONCLUSION

G od has called you, not only to salvation, but he called you to a total relationship with him and for the purposes, he had for us from before the foundation of the world. As we evaluate his call, he causes us to want to do his will, and then he enables us to do it. Understand this, his call to a relationship with him has provided all we need to live fully with him. His call will always involve us in his redemptive activity, and he will work through us in this world. We have come to know God and grow toward Christlikeness. And with that being said, a Christlike character is the method he uses to prepare for eternity with him. Suffice it to say, God has a plan and a purpose for each one of us! So, now respond to his call as he works in you mightily in this world.

The key all of us need to understand is that the greatest privileges are given freely to every believer.

As you move forward in your Christian life, I urge you to learn how to establish a regular quiet time with the Father through prayer and begin a Bible study on your own or in a group, whether at church or through other Christian friends. Make it a point to become a member of a Bible-believing, Bible-preaching, and Bible practicing church. Seek God's direction for your life and utilize the opportunities he gives you to share the gospel with lost friends.

There is an old hymn we used to sing titled "Give of Your Best to the Master" by Charlotte A. Barnard (1863) and the opening words say this:

> *"Give of your best to the Master;*
> *Give of the strength of your youth;*
> *Throw your soul's fresh, glowing*
> *ardor*
> *Into the battle for truth.*
> *Jesus has set the example,*
> *Dauntless was He, young and*
> *brave;*
> *Give Him your loyal devotion;*
> *Give Him the best that you have.*
>
> *Refrain:*
> *Give of your best to the Master;*
> *Give of the strength of your youth;*
> *Clad in salvation's full armor,*
> *Join in the battle for truth."*

May God richly bless you in your journey through your Christian life.

Heavenly Father, I pray for the reader of this book. May you bless him or her in their journey of life with You. Guide them closely and speak to their hearts daily. I pray for him or her to apply these tools in their everyday life. I pray all this in the precious name of Jesus our Lord. Amen.

BOB LANKFORD

ABOUT THE AUTHOR

Bob Lankford is a retired Baptist pastor who entered ministry late in life at the age of thirty-seven. He worked in banking and finance before moving into the manufacturing field, promoting up to supervisory ranks for several years. Ministry was the furthest thing from his mind, when the Lord finally began to work in his life, eventually calling him into full-time gospel ministry.

Bob and his wife Deanna and two children, Stephanie and Brian packed up everything they had, sold their house, and moved to Ft. Worth, TX where he would attend Southwestern Baptist Theological Seminary to pursue an Associate of Divinity degree in 1984. Upon graduating in 1987, he was called to his first pastorate in Sanderson, TX. After completing pastorates in Sanderson, TX, Wilson, TX, and Lubbock, TX, he was called to Melrose, NM before moving to Fountain Inn, SC where he eventually retired from ministry and moved back to Texas. He and Deanna ended up in Denison, Texas near Lake Texoma where they bought a home and settled down.

God laid on Bob's heart to write. He wrote daily devotions and was published in David C. Cook's publication of *Devotions* magazine. Bob has had a heart for discipleship and helping new

Christians get settled into a daily routine of Bible study and prayer. God led him to write a book for new Christians, and those returning to the faith, with the tools needed for building a strong Christian life. Fiction is also something he is working on. He does have a mystery book still in progress and he is now looking forward to returning to that book and whatever else the Lord lays on his heart to write.

Bob is also the leader of Texoma Christian Writers Group which has only just begun. You can keep up with Bob's blogs at his author's website www.boblankford.com. You can sign up for his monthly newsletter at his site as well.